Also by Martha Graybeal Rowlett:

In Spirit and in Truth
(Upper Room Books, 1982)

Responding to God: A Guide to Daily Prayer
(Upper Room Books, 1996)

Leader's Guide: Responding to God
(Upper Room Books, 2000)

Praying Together: Forming Prayer Ministries in Your Congregation
(Upper Room Books, 2002)

Weaving Prayer Into the Tapestry of Life

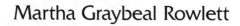

Martha Graybeal Rowlett

WestBow
PRESS
A DIVISION OF THOMAS NELSON

WestBow Press books may be ordered through booksellers or by contacting:
WestBow Press
A Division of Thomas Nelson
1663 Liberty Drive
Bloomington, IN 47403
www.westbowpress.com
1-(866) 928-1240

ISBN: 978-1-4497-9516-0 (sc)
ISBN: 978-1-4497-9515-3 (hc)
ISBN: 978-1-4497-9517-7 (e)
Library of Congress Control Number: 2013908795

Printed in the United States of America.
WestBow Press rev. date: 06/26/2013

To the staff at Givens Estates in Asheville, North Carolina, in appreciation for their commitment to supporting residents in weaving beautiful life tapestries in the senior years of life.

Table of Contents

Preface

I was fresh out of seminary and newly ordained as a minister when the bishop gave me a surprising challenge. He sent me to be the associate pastor at a large, sophisticated congregation in Palo Alto, California, where one of my first assignments was to prepare and lead the prayers for congregational worship every week. I was their first woman pastor and was eager to make a good impression and do a good job. This task forced me to confront the poverty of my own experience with prayer. My seminary offered no courses on prayer. My personal experience of prayer was to thank God spontaneously for something beautiful or pleasant or to call out to God for help in trouble when no other solution seemed readily available. I knew how to do almost everything else the associate pastor job required. But nobody warned me about this.

I began researching the experience of prayer in the Christian church. I discovered a rich and wonderful tradition of which I had been only superficially aware. Preparing to lead this congregation in corporate prayer each week led to significant personal spiritual growth for me. Before long, I realized that the way one prays grows out of the way one thinks about God. This new assignment put pressure on my theology. I was pushed to ask myself questions about the nature of the One with whom I was communicating in prayer. I asked myself, "What am I doing here in giving voice to the prayers of these people?"

The most helpful resources for this pilgrimage came from the writings of two men, both named John. The first was Dr. John

Magee. He led a prayer retreat for our church. I eagerly read his book *Reality and Prayer*. He introduced me to what he called "the spectrum of prayer." He believed that prayer, like white sunlight, is one. But as there are many colors in that white light, so there are many kinds of prayer, all "a colorful fragment of the whole." My personal prayers burst out of the bonds of saying "thank you" and "help me." I developed a pattern that still guides me into a far richer experience of God's gift of prayer.

Dr. John Cobb came to my rescue in the struggle with thinking about God. I found my faith home in reading a chapter in his book *God and the World*. His ideas fit my worldview and my personal experience and just felt like the truth. I was fortunate a few years later to work with Dr. Cobb in writing a theology of prayer for my project for the doctor of ministry degree at Claremont School of Theology.

Dr. Cobb suggested that I write for publication for lay people. Materials at the core of that project were published by the Upper Room in 1982 as *In Spirit and in Truth*. These materials were revised and expanded and published in 1996 as *Responding to God: A Guide to Daily Prayer*.

I am now retired from active ministry. The journey launched in Palo Alto grows better with the years. I don't think my senior pastor gave much thought to the assignment he handed to his new associate, but it has been life-transforming for me. My understanding of and experience with prayer continues to grow. The image of weaving prayer into the tapestry of life has special meaning to me now that I have more years to remember than years to anticipate.

This is a new book. I included in the earlier books some prayer phrases that reflected the spectrum of prayer I have used to provide structure for personal prayer. I am using that same format here because I know people who keep these books handy to use on a regular basis. This time they are called Prayer Prompts, and one set accompanies each chapter. But the contents of *Weaving Prayer into the Tapestry of Life* reflect sixteen additional years of living and learning since the publication of *Responding to God.*

The audience is still both the novice in prayer and the experienced pray-er who is interested in expanding and deepening a personal experience of prayer.

My deepest appreciation goes out to John Cobb for suggesting that I share this pilgrimage by writing. My husband, Bob Arnott, shared generously his practical wisdom and warm confidence, literally making possible my writing adventures. My brother, Pete Rowlett, and sister-in-law, Ginny Rowlett, have been cheerleaders and energetic supporters of my writing projects. My pastors, Guy Sayles and Rob Blackburn, have nurtured the flame of faith with outstanding preaching that will be echoed unmistakably in these pages. All of the people who have shared their faith journeys with me in classes and retreats and small groups deserve a standing ovation for the enrichment their openness and candor has provided. My neighbor John Nieburg has generously and graciously provided technical support to link my computer and the world of digital communication. I also thank Martha Brown, Rufus Stark, Martha Black, and Suzanne DePree for manuscript reviews and helpful suggestions.

I Come To Prayer

I come to prayer eager to:
- open my heart and mind to God.
- feel that wholeness of the Spirit who is my true nature and destiny.
- be enabled to look to the future with a serene confidence.
- be aware that my frailty does not matter.
- realize that I am infinitely cherished.

I come to prayer seeking to:
- come to my senses in the presence of your holy love.
- catch my breath in the presence of your pure beauty.
- join my human love in a chorus of wonder and praise.
- gather anything that is true and holy within me.
- be alive with love and gratitude in my whole being.[1]

INTRODUCTION

Setting up the Loom

As a deer longs for flowing streams,
so my soul longs for you, O God.
Psalm 42:1

B ooks, like people, have personalities. Some books are an easy,
fun read, ideal for a rainy Saturday afternoon or a day at the
beach. Page-turners keep you awake until three in the morning.
"Life changers" give you insight or information that answers
important questions. Books can scare you or thrill you or inform
you. Books can be boring. After a few pages, you yawn and close
the book, and that's that.

With most books, once you have read the last page, you can put
them on the shelf or pass them on to someone else. Those books are
like visitors. They come and go. This book wants to hang around
and be used. It would like to be a friendly companion to help you
connect with God about the living of your life as you weave your
personal life tapestry

The chapters of this book talk about prayer. They provide an
overview of a Christian understanding and practice of prayer.

While leading retreats, classes, and workshops, I have
discovered that many people have unanswered questions about

prayer. Some confess that these questions dampen their enthusiasm about praying. Others admit that intellectual challenges block them from praying, except in times of crisis, of course! Our worldview has been shaped by the scientific revolution of the past two hundred years. For many people, prayer has become a meaningless vestige of the past because it defies critical scientific analysis. They see it as existing in the shadowy realm of magic and superstition. Others continue to go through the motions of prayer, but they are not sure what they are doing. Some whose prayers are limited to asking give up on prayer if their expectations are not met.

The chapters of this book offer my personal conclusions out of a struggle to create a thinking person's faith in prayer. Chapter 1 sets the context with an image of life as weaving. Chapter 2 looks at the thread of prayer, with special attention to what we can believe about the One with whom we commune in prayer. With the loom set up, the rest of the book explores the forms the thread of prayer can take in our life weaving. As we create the tapestry of our lives, we can ask God for ourselves and others. We can deal with the past. We can listen to what God would say to us. We can respond to God. The last two chapters look at ways Christians pray together and summarize some of the difference prayer makes.

After each chapter, there is an invitation to move from thinking to doing. A series of "Prayer Prompts" provide a structure for experiencing all of the dimensions of Christian prayer discussed in the book.

I created the first set of prayer prompts to provide a structure for expanding my private prayer experience into the wider world of Christian prayer. I have shared these guides for prayer with others who have found them helpful. The general outline of a set of prayer prompts leads you through the following kinds of prayer:

1. Centering
2. Praise
3. Confession

4. Meditative reading of Scripture
5. Petition
6. Intercession
7. Thanksgiving
8. Dedication
9. Silence
10. Benediction

Short phrases in each section that end in an ellipse (...) invite you to complete the thought with whatever rises from your heart. For example, a passage of praise from a psalm will be followed by "I praise you for..." A brief prayer of confession will conclude with, "I confess..." These phrases, often from Scripture and Christian tradition and practice, will help you get started with your own prayer. These prayer prompts can be adapted for long-term use. (This is the "hanging around" part!)

Seven Scripture passages are listed at the end of each set of prayer prompts. They relate to the content of the chapters and have the same theme. They may be used for the meditative reading of Scripture in your private prayer or as an enrichment resource for group study of this book.

If you use the prayer prompts as you go through the book, they will provide experience on which to reflect when you look at these dimensions of prayer in more detail in later chapters.

A journal or notebook in which you write your prayers may be helpful. The prompts pages do not provide enough room for you to write in your own prayers. A record of your prayers in a journal may produce interesting insights as you review later what you have been praying. You may see a difference your prayers have made. You may discover how your prayers have grown and assumed new shapes as you prayed them. You may want to record some of these insights in your journal as well. You will need to use a Bible in the meditative reading of the Scripture section of the prayer guide.

Some of the forms of prayer may feel awkward at first. Give them a try. You may like them!

The use of these prayer prompts to provide a framework for your praying will help the reading come alive. Our prayers can go where our thoughts about prayer cannot follow.

You don't need to do the whole sequence of prayers every time you want to pray. Sometimes you will need just to confess or to give thanks or to intercede for someone. You may want to add additional resources in a journal or notebook that are helpful in leading you into the miraculous dialogue with God.

A passage from the worship resources of Bruce Prewer of Australia will open each set of prayer prompts.

A word of encouragement: Martin Luther once said, "None can believe how powerful prayer is, and what it is able to effect, but those who have learned it by experience."[2] The primary way a person grows in the experience of prayer is by praying. *Weaving Prayer into the Tapestry of Life* can help that happen for you.

And a disclaimer: St. Teresa of Avila has been quoted as saying that the best way to pray is the way you pray best. Each of us needs to create an approach that seems natural and that fits where we are. The pattern used here reflects centuries of experience in Christian devotion. This pattern is only one of the many possible options and is offered here as a learning experience.

PRAYER PROMPTS I
Introduction

I come to prayer eager to open my heart and mind to God.

Centering
As a deer longs for flowing streams, so my soul longs for you, O God.[3]

It's me, it's me, it's me, O Lord, standing in the need of prayer...[4]

Praise
This is a day, an hour, a moment that you have made, O Lord. I give you thanks for this opportunity to be alive and to praise you for who you are and what you do...

Joyful, joyful, we adore you, God of glory, Lord of Love; hearts unfold like flowers before you, opening to the sun above.[5]

I praise you...

Confession

Everybody sins and falls short of what you call us to be. As I turn my attention to your presence with me, I am aware that this is true of me, even on my best days. I deeply regret opportunities to do your will that I have missed and hurt or damage I have caused. I confess that I have not lived the way you would have me to live in these ways...

Forgive me, O God, and in your grace give me a fresh start.

When you ask, God will grant you remission of all your sins and the grace and peace of the Holy Spirit.

Meditative Reading of Scripture
(See passages listed below featuring Jesus and prayer.)

Petitions (Prayers for Oneself)

As Jesus asked for guidance when he had a decision to make, so also I ask you for guidance at this point where I have a decision to make...

As Jesus shared with you the pain in his life, so I share with you my pain, asking for relief from suffering...

As Jesus taught his disciples to pray, I ask you to teach me to pray...

I pray for...

Intercession (Prayers for Others)

As Jesus blessed the children, so also I ask your blessing for children. I pray for the children of the world, with all of their potential and vulnerability. I share with you my concerns and my hopes for particular children...

As Jesus prayed for his friends, so also I pray for my friends. I pray that they may know your peace that passes our human understanding and respond faithfully to your call in their lives. Today I remember...

As Jesus prayed for his enemies, so I pray for those who cause me pain and difficulty. May the tangled relationships be unraveled and the wounds healed, and through the miracle of your grace, may we become friends. I pray for...

I pray for...

Thanksgiving

Gracious God, I am thankful for all your goodness to me and to all of your creation. I thank you for creating, preserving, and blessing my life. I thank you for the gift of salvation in Jesus Christ, for the ways you continue to sustain and guide me in every day, and for the hope you make possible.[6]

I thank you for...

Dedication

This little light of mine, I'm goin' a let it shine,
Everywhere I go, I'm goin' a let it shine,
Let it shine, let it shine, let it shine.[7]

I will let my light shine in this way...

Silence

Benediction

Go in the faith that the presence of God within you will give you strength to confront any challenge that is before you.

Scripture Passages for Meditative Reading or for Group Study

Passages reporting on Jesus in prayer:
  Luke 6:12–16
  Mark 14:32–42
  Luke 11:1–4
  Luke 23:44–46
  Matthew 19:13–15
  Luke 22:31–32
  Luke 23:32–35

CHAPTER 1

Living as Weaving

See, I am making all things new.
Revelation 21:5

A large tapestry hangs on the wall of my living room. The design features a bouquet of flowers in a marble urn. Threads in subtle shades of green, red, gray, gold, pink, brown, peach, blue, and ivory are woven together to create a picture. From many threads has come one design.

Living is like weaving. In every moment of every day, we bring together many threads to create one life. Everybody does it.

The threads that create the design of your life come from three major sources:

1. the past,
2. the possibilities for the future that God offers, and
3. your free will.

You consciously connect what is going on right now (the past) with what God wants for you (the possibilities) when you weave prayer into the tapestry of your life. You choose (use your free will) to include God's vision in the design of the life tapestry you are weaving.

The center of the action in weaving a life tapestry is always *right now*. As you wake to begin each new day, you wake to the flow of the future becoming the past. The future is not yet here. The past is already done and set. You weave your life moment by moment with the threads that are at hand. When you weave prayer into the tapestry of your life, you use your free will to consciously involve God's vision of possibilities for you as you move from the past to the future.

If you want to weave prayer into the tapestry of your life, where do you begin? Like a weaver, you begin with what has already been done—the work completed on the loom. A design is already there. You have threads already woven in and ready for you to take up and use in this day's weaving. As we think about weaving your life, the work already done can be called the past.

The Past

The starting place for each day's weaving is the person you are in that moment.

You are a product of both ancient history and recent history—in fact, very ancient history and very recent history and everything in between. Your past is not just what you did yesterday or a decision you made ten years ago. You are an expression of all of life. Your history goes back into the mystery that surrounds the beginning of all things. You are not only weaving the tapestry of your own life. You are also engaged in the larger process of weaving the ongoing story of creation as part of a vast, interconnected universe.

Current events in your life are also part of your past. By the time they affect you, they have happened and are set. No backspace, delete, or undo key can change the fact that someone has just rear-ended your car at a traffic light. Your weaving in this moment will have to incorporate this accident from the immediate past. A surprise promotion on the job will instantly modify your design. Your reaction to that news itself becomes in the next moment a part of your past. Your past is the state of the whole universe as it affects you personally in the present moment.

When you were born, many dimensions of who you are were already set. Your DNA, your racial/ethnic/national heritage, your innate personality orientation, and your family history were there before you began to exercise your free will. You began life with a significant past.

Martin Luther King Jr. was born in 1929 into a black, deeply religious family in the American South. He had natural gifts for leadership and public speaking. His ancestors had sung hymns about freedom from slavery. A brightening vision of a future of racial equality in America was stirring in the world around him as he grew up. His life tapestry was evolving so that he was ready to change history with his "I Have a Dream" speech when the opportunity came in 1963.

On a less-dramatic scale, my family history with Methodist ancestors on both sides for several generations back powerfully influenced me. My early past began in a Methodist congregation and a Methodist extended family. I was enrolled in a Methodist church nursery department before I was a month old. I did not learn about Presbyterians and Baptists—to say nothing of Buddhists, Hindus, Muslims, and Jews—for years to come. Threads of Methodism were ready for my weaving. When I was ready to be ordained as a minister, the threads going back to the nursery class strongly influenced my choice to take this step in my family's faith community.

Decisions you have made, your education, habits you have formed, talents and skills you have developed, and relationships you have cultivated are all part of the constantly evolving package of your past.

Circumstances beyond your control are continually affecting your weaving. Good teachers can help children learn, abusive parents can cause permanent damage, and an accident or a serious illness can cause a radical change of design. Residents of a city devastated by a major earthquake immediately lose many threads with which they had been weaving. Suddenly they have a new set of threads to weave. Everything else is still there in the life tapestry design created up to this moment, but possibilities for the future will be quite different.

Your past changes moment by moment. Your past brings you to the center of the weaving action—the present moment.

This is where we hear the call of God.

The Call of God

In setting up the loom of creation, God has included God's self everywhere. Creation was not a one-time event. Creation is an ongoing process, and God is right in the middle of it.

This means at the personal level that God is present to you in every second of your existence. God is both beyond you and within you continuing the process of creation in you and through you. Other threads may come and go in different stages of your life, but the opportunity for communion between your spirit and God's Spirit is always available.

I am fond of a phrase used by Jean-Pierre de Caussade, a French Jesuit teacher and writer in the eighteenth century. "The sacrament of the present moment,"[8] he said, is where God can be found. God is right there offering possibilities for the future as you move out of the past.

The nature of God's activity is described in the Scriptures as love. As an expression of that love, God has created ideal possibilities for everything. God is actively calling all creation to fulfill these possibilities.

DeCaussade speaks of "God's treasury," which faith unlocks. In God's treasury are all the possibilities for the maximum well-being of the creation. God is not a great cosmic Santa Claus to whom we come with a list or the great vending machine in the sky with buttons for all the goodies we might want. But God does desire that we realize the potential of each moment of our existence. God calls us into a future of possibility. God presents to us in every moment the ideal potential for where we are now.

The possibilities God offers us change moment by moment. God adapts the ideal possibilities offered to us to fit where we are now, even as our past continually changes by incorporating the outcomes of each present moment.

The decisions we make close off some options and open up others. For example, if as a teenager I had chosen to marry my high school sweetheart, this would have opened up a new range of opportunities I did not have as a single person. At the same time, I would have closed the door on other sets of possibilities open to me. If, however, I had chosen to focus my attention on a professional career and not marry until I was middle-aged, I would have had a very different set of opportunities and closed doors.

Even minor decisions impact what God can offer as ideal possibilities for the next moment.

While the specifics of what God can offer as ideal possibilities change in each new moment, the overall purposes of God in creation remain the same. Alfred North Whitehead, writing in *Process and Reality,* describes God as "the poet of the world, with tender patience leading it by his vision of truth, beauty, and goodness."[9] God goes before us with the ideal possibilities for us and meets us as we weave, seeking to lure us on in the direction of God's eternal purposes.

We cannot escape our past or change it. But there is always hope for what comes next because of God's activity in us and among us.

Free Will

The easiest course in weaving in each moment is to let the past determine the future and to go with the flow.

The vast past does not necessarily control what we do because we have been given the gift of free will. God has set up the loom of life so a great deal of creation has at least a small degree of capacity for self-determination. You are more than simply what you have been. Space for making choices about how you will respond to what the past gives you is part of your created nature. You have freedom to choose in each all-important moment what you will do with the threads from your past—how you will use those threads and where you will go from here.

There are always limits on our freedom of will. Both the structures of creation and your particular past give you limited options for choice. You cannot choose to get pregnant and give birth to a child if you were formed in the womb as a male. You cannot run for mayor of the city in this year's election if you were born only eight years ago. You cannot choose to live to be 150 years old. If you have not finished high school, you cannot choose to obtain a license to practice medicine before going to school for many more years. Still, the human capacity to choose is very powerful in spite of its limits.

Victor Frankl, a Jewish psychiatrist from Vienna, gives a vivid picture of the power of free will in his book *Man's Search for Meaning*. He spent four years in the dehumanizing conditions of a Nazi concentration camp in Germany during World War II. Prisoners faced the daily threat of death in the gas chamber. They were beaten, worked as slave labor in all kinds of weather, fed a starvation diet, and housed in crowded tents. Many simply gave up and died. Others, including Frankl, chose to keep their spirits alive by remembering who they were and by thinking about what they hoped to do when the horror ended. Frankl survived to write a book about the experience and to begin a new school of psychotherapy based on what he learned from the ordeal. His suffering was transformed into a source of healing for others.

Knowing the right choice to make is not always simple. What design comes next? What threads should I put where? Do I need to drop a thread or add a thread? We don't always make the right decisions, even when we know the right choice. The inner strength to choose the right option is not always there.

The jokes we hear every January about New Year's resolutions and their dismal history of failure remind us that the exercise of free will is not simple or easy. The influence of the past is strong. You may will with the best intentions to lose weight, but deeply ingrained habits of eating (the past) may find you greeting the next New Year heavier rather than lighter.

The Bible is full of stories of the human struggle with free will. In fact, the Bible begins with a story about it. The creation story in Genesis 2 is about Adam and Eve and the snake deciding what they are going to do about that tempting apple hanging low on the tree in the garden of Eden. God put them in a dream location that was blessed with wonderful possibilities for an abundant life. God had launched a beautiful design, but it was a design that included the freedom to make choices about what to do with this incredible gift. Adam and Eve exercised their free will, ate the forbidden apple, and were thrown out of the Garden.

The apostle Paul, writing to the church in Rome in a letter preserved in the New Testament, confessed his own struggles with free will: "I do not understand my own actions. For I do not do what I want, but I do the very thing I hate" (Romans 7:15). I can will what is right, but I cannot do it" (Romans 7:18). Paul attributed this to sin (Romans 7–8). He was caught between his old lifestyle as a Roman citizen and his new lifestyle as a Christian. The past was pulling his weaving each day in the old directions, but now he felt the powerful pull of God to weave a new design for his life. He spoke out in anguish: "Wretched man that I am! Who will rescue me from this body of death (Romans 7:24)?" Then he proclaimed: "The law of the Spirit of life in Christ Jesus has set you free from the law of sin and of death" (Romans 8:2). Later he said, "For those who live according to the flesh set their minds on the things of the flesh, but those who live according to the Spirit, set their minds on the things of the Spirit. ...to set the mind on the Spirit is life and peace"(Romans 8:5-6).

Paul discovered the secret that makes the difference. To "set the mind on the things of the Spirit" could be a definition of prayer. When you use your free will to choose to weave prayer into the tapestry of your life, you open yourself to the guidance and power of God's Spirit with you.

The story of Nelson Mandela in South Africa illustrates the difference the thread of prayer can make. South Africa had a deeply entrenched social structure of apartheid. But the past of that nation was confronted by the call of God to a new system, with justice and freedom for all citizens. Mandela, a man of deep spirituality, emerged as the leader who could articulate that vision for the masses of people around the world who also heard this call. The influence of the past was formidable, but the persuasive power of the ideal possibility God was offering through the life and witness of Mandela was stronger. Mandela used his free will to respond to God's call to a better future.

The call of God is not always a pleasant experience. Sometimes we, like many people in South Africa, want to stay where we are and let the past shape the future. Mandela's choice to embody the vision led him to spend many years in prison. We may be willing to grow toward "God's vision of truth, beauty and goodness" as long as the path is easy and pleasant. Even Jesus asked to be relieved of the pain of the cross. But when God's call leads us through hard times, we can trust that our part of the larger tapestry of creation will be used to express God's love for all creation.

You open yourself to the presence of God's Spirit when you choose to weave the thread of prayer into the tapestry of your life. Welcoming God's Spirit into your life brings you the gifts of God's grace and power. These gifts can enable you to add to the ongoing design of God's creation expressions of God's love.

Conclusion

My tapestry is the first thing people see when they come into the front door of my home. They often stop to admire it. The tapestry is a thing of beauty. I see the tapestry as a metaphor of God's will for the world and for each of our lives. God would have all living things take the variety of threads available to them and create beauty to be enjoyed.

The tapestry on my wall is finished. The design is complete. But the weaving of God's creation is still in process. You are one of the weavers in God's ongoing creation for at least as long as you live.

PRAYER PROMPTS 2
Living as Weaving

I come to prayer eager to feel the wholeness of
the Spirit that is my true nature and destiny.

Centering

See, I am making all things new.[10]
God is present in the world today, making new the whole creation.
I will be glad in this day…
Lord, I turn from the activities and preoccupations that absorb my
life to spend time with you…

Praise

With the psalmist, I ask in wonder:
God, brilliant Lord, I look up at your macro-skies,
dark and enormous, your handmade sky-jewelry,
Moon and stars mounted in their settings.
Then I look at my micro-self and wonder,
Why do you bother with us? Why take a second look our way?
You put us in charge of your handcrafted world.[11]
And you offer us the relationship of prayer.

With the psalmist, my heart is filled with awe in your presence. I
praise you for…

Confession

Almighty God, to you all hearts are open, all desires known, and from you no secrets are hidden. Cleanse the thoughts of my heart by the inspiration of your Holy Spirit, so that I may perfectly love and serve and honor you through Christ our Lord.[12]

I confess that the thoughts of my heart need to be cleansed today in these ways...

If we confess our sins, God is faithful and just, and will forgive us.[13]

Meditative Reading of Scripture
(See passages listed below.)

Petition

I pray for the healing of my body, my mind, and my spirit. Help me to do my part in releasing the springs of health you have placed in me. I pray for...

I pray for strength in my inner being as I confront this challenging part of my life...

Lift my vision beyond the boundaries of my small, self-centered world to the wider horizon of your hopes for this world. Show me the ideas, possibilities, relationships and understandings that are your will for me...

I pray for...

Intercessions

I pray for my community, that good may triumph over evil, that love may conquer hate. I pray especially for this need in my community...

I pray for my family, especially for this person with a special need...

I pray for the church. Touch us with the wonder of Christ's love, and send us out into the world to do what he would do. I pray especially for...

I pray for...

Thanksgiving

When upon life's billows you are tempest tossed,
When you are discouraged, thinking all is lost,
Count your many blessings, name them one by one,
And it will surprise you what the Lord hath done.
Count your blessings, name them one by one,
Count your blessings, see what God hath done!
Count your blessings, name them one by one,
And it will surprise you what the Lord hath done.[14]
I give thanks to you for the gifts of the past that bless me still today. Today I thank you for...

Dedication

The Prayer of St. Francis

Lord, make me an instrument of your peace,
where there is hatred, let me sow love;

where there is injury, pardon;
where there is doubt, faith; where there is despair, hope;
where there is darkness, light; where there is sadness, joy.
O Divine Master, grant that I may not so much seek to be consoled
as to console;
to be understood as to understand; to be loved as to love;
for it is in giving that we receive,
it is in pardoning that we are pardoned,
and it is in dying that we are born to eternal life.
Lord, I pray that you will use me in this way...

Silence

Benediction

Glory be to the Father and to the Son and to the Holy Spirit; as it was
in the beginning, is now, and ever shall be, world without end.[15]

Scripture Passages for Meditative Reading or for Group Study

Passages about the call of God:

    Genesis 1:1–31

    Genesis 12:1–2

    Exodus 3:1–15

    Jeremiah 1:4–10

    Luke 1:26–38

    Luke 4:16–21

    Acts 9:1–19

CHAPTER 2

The Thread of Prayer

Be still and know that I am God.
Isaiah 46:10

Prayer is a gift of love from God that is available to everybody all of the time and everywhere. Other threads may come and go, but prayer is always there as a resource for your weaving.

Prayer does not always look the same. People weaving prayer into their life tapestries may be kneeling with head bowed, eyes closed, and hands folded. They may be lying in bed, walking, digging in the garden, or dancing. A praying person may be using words or being silent, singing or chanting. People pray alone and with each other. Together in worship services they may pray with ancient prayers in formal liturgies or with spontaneous prayers. Prayer can be joyful or anguished.

Prayer is not a one-size-fits-all gift. God meets us where we are. The story is told of a man who regularly spent an hour each day sitting in the front row of a small chapel in his town. One day the priest met him as he left and asked him what he did each day in the chapel. The man pointed to the crucifix on the altar before which he sat and said, "I just look at him, and he looks at me." God was meeting him there in his silent looking.

People who regularly weave the thread of prayer into their

lives describe the experience in their own unique way. I have a fascinating collection of definitions of prayer. Three of my favorites reveal responses to God's gift from three different personalities. Mother Teresa is matter-of-fact: "Prayer is simply talking to God," she says. "He speaks to us. We listen. We speak to him. He listens."[16] Fredrich Heiler, in his book *Prayer*, is poetic. Prayer is "a mysterious linking of the human and the divine... an incomprehensible wonder, a miracle of miracles."[17] Archbishop Desmond Tutu speaks from his heart and describes prayer as like warming oneself before the glow of God. [18]

To me, prayer is all of the above and more, but my working definition is, "Prayer is conscious, intentional communion between a human being and God." Webster's dictionary defines communion as "an intimate relationship with deep understanding." To go one more step with the dictionary, Webster's first definition of "intimate" is "pertaining to the inmost character of a thing, fundamental." Prayer can be understood as a conscious, intentional relationship between the inmost character of a person and the inmost character of God with deep understanding.

The word *openness* is for me a quick way to say "conscious, intentional communion."

Prayer as Openness

Mother Teresa describes this openness as being two-way. God talks; we listen. We talk; God listens. Jesus organized the model prayer he gave the disciples on this two-way pattern. He begins as a listener to God.

> Our Father in heaven, hallowed be your name.
> Your Kingdom come. Your will be done, on earth
> as it is in heaven.

These first three of the six phrases in this prayer have the human side in listening mode to who God is and what God wants.

Then Jesus speaks, asking God for the necessities of life, for forgiveness, and for protection.

> Give us this day our daily bread. And forgive us our debts, as we also have forgiven our debtors. And do not bring us to the time of trial, but rescue us from the evil one. (Matthew 6: 9–13)

Mother Teresa has learned how to pray from Jesus, and we can too!

The thread of prayer is like a phone call that carries messages back and forth between two parties in conscious, intentional communion with each other. As a two-way dialogue, prayer is openness *to* God and *with* God.

Let's look first at the side of this communication with which most of us have the least experience: God talking.

Prayer as Openness *to* God

Private prayers sometimes jump over the listening part of the model prayer and head straight for the requesting part. Prayer becomes significantly impoverished when we are the center of our own attention and God is just the audience—the one who is expected to provide what is asked. God's gift of love offered in the relationship of prayer is diminished when the gift of God's presence is ignored.

Most Christian worship services take seriously the structure of the Lord's Prayer and begin with calls to worship and songs of praise. Attention is given to who God is, what God is doing, and what God wants. The prayer prompts at the end of each chapter in this book begin this way. This first response of openness *to* God serves as orientation for the rest of the prayer experience.

One of the hymns of the church speaks of God as "immortal, invisible, God only wise, in light inaccessible, hid from our eyes."[19] Our thoughts can never stretch around the nature and being of God. But the Christian faith is that we can know enough to be able to receive the gift of prayer. Two affirmations about God in our Christian heritage give us a rich picture of the other person on the phone call. Simply stated, these are: God is with us, and God is love.

God Is with Us

Primitive images of God usually have located God out there somewhere. Some religious language assumes distance between oneself and God. For Christians, God is certainly beyond creation, but God is also within all of creation. God is present everywhere all of the time. God can be thought of as with you and within you always.

Jean-Pierre de Caussaude, in talking about the "sacrament of the present moment," used phrases like "every fraction of a second" and "into the very marrow of your bones"[20] to talk about how close God is to us. You don't have to look around for God or call for God to come when you want to pray. God can't come any closer!

The heart has been described as the location of God's presence, perhaps because it has been thought of as the source of life, the core of a person's being. So we sing, "Into my heart, into my heart, come into my heart, Lord Jesus." With the increasing familiarity with the physical heart and all of its chambers and valves and functions, some people prefer other terms, like "ground of our being" or "essence of being" or "soul," to refer to God's presence with us and God's image within us.

Thomas Kelly, in his *Testament of Devotion,* used the word *soul*: "Deep within us all there is an amazing inner sanctuary of the soul, a holy place, a Divine Center, a speaking Voice, to which we continuously return."[21]

When you want to begin your prayer with openness to God, you can just turn on and tune in. No busy signals or voicemails or electronic snafus interfere. God is ready and available when you are.

But you are not the only one. God is with the whole creation, offering this gift of loving presence. Your inner world is connected through a shared presence with all that is when you are open to

God in prayer. You can lift your eyes from the distortions of your limited self-interest and look at reality from the perspective of God. The relationship of prayer can be already changing you before any words are said when you begin prayer with openness *to* God.

God knows everything that has been or currently is. God has been everywhere all of the time through history and so has firsthand experience. Many centuries ago, the psalmist sang about God's complete knowledge:

> O Lord, you have searched me and known me. You know when I sit down and when I rise up; you discern my thoughts from far away. You search out my path and my lying down, and are acquainted with all my ways. Even before a word is on my tongue, O Lord, you know it completely. You hem me in, behind and before, and lay your hand upon me. Such knowledge is too wonderful for me; it is so high that I cannot attain it… For it was you who formed my inward parts; you knit me together in my mother's womb. I praise you, for I am fearfully and wonderfully made (Psalm 139: 1–6, 13–14).

When you pray, you can trust that God knows you behind all of your self-doubts, anxieties, pretensions, masks, and roles. God knows the essential you in a way you can never fully know yourself. God is aware of your circumstances from a perspective you cannot share. You are not spending time with a stranger or a casual acquaintance when you pray with openness to God. No introductions are necessary. God is up-to-date about everything.

Matthew refers to two sayings of Jesus connecting our praying to God's knowledge of everything that can be known. He says to his disciples, "Your Father knows what you need before you ask him" (Matthew 6:8). Later, he says to them, "Even the hairs of your head are all counted" (Matthew 10:30). The clear implication is that God knows you better than you know yourself. Very few of us (only the completely bald!) can report accurately on the number of hairs on our heads.

The God who is present to you in each moment also knows what is available for the future. God—the one who created all that is—knows the possibilities available in every moment.

You open yourself to coming to know the possibilities for you when you open yourself to God in prayer.

The God who is with you is actively creating. God is not just sitting around keeping an eye on things. God is weaving the whole creation, taking its past into an ever-new future.

A clergywoman neighbor, Mary Caldwell, tells about a conversation with her four-year-old son, who asked one day, "What is the last number?" She responded, "Only God knows." He came back a few days later to report. "I don't think there is a last number. God is still making numbers."[22]

The God who is with you now is actively creating and ready to work with you in your weaving as you move from the past to the future.

God Is Love

The Bible tells a consistent story from Genesis to Revelation. God, the creator, loves the creation. Where God is, God loves. This is not just a matter of positive feelings. The one who made all that is stays involved, willing good for everything and everybody.

You open yourself to this love when you open yourself to communion with God. You make room for this love to be in your life design when you weave the thread of prayer into your life tapestry. Bishop Tutu talks about his experience of God:

> I have come to realize more and more that prayer
> is just being in the presence of one who loves you
> deeply, who loves you with a love that will not let
> you go, and so when I get up in the morning I try

to spend as much time as I can in the sense of being
quiet in the presence of this love. It's like I'm sitting
in front of a warm fire on a cold day. I don't have to
do anything. All I have to do is be there. And after
a while, I may have the qualities of the fire change
me so I have the warmth of the fire. I may have the
glow of the fire, and it is so also with me and God.
I just have to be there, quiet.[23]

John Cobb and David Griffin helpfully suggest that you can
think of God's love in two ways: as creative love and as responsive
love.[24] God's creative love is God's original intention for everything
to be good. God's responsive love is what God has to do because
things don't always go the way God wants.

God's Creative Love

A God of love is a God who can be trusted to want the best for
all the objects of that love. You can ask God for what you need and
expect that God's answer will be good. This also means you can
join Jesus in praying, "Your will be done."

A trusting prayer can be a humble prayer. God's love is better
than our human love. God's love is a pure love, while our human
love sometimes has complicating factors. God knows better about
what is needed anywhere, anytime than any human being can
know. Telling God in no uncertain terms what you want done in
any situation and expecting an answer that precisely matches the
request misses the opportunity to be open to God's good will. God's
awareness of the ideal possibilities in any situation is better than
our insight. Our prayers for ourselves and others can be trusting,
humble communion.

Openness to a God of love in the relationship of prayer can also
be an occasion for joy and thanksgiving. You can find hope and
peace just by turning your attention to the wonder of who God is
and what God has done and is doing. A day can be changed, a life

transformed without any words being used. One of my favorite prayer phrases says, "I come to prayer eager to come to my senses in the presence of your holy love."[25] Time spent in openness *to* God who is actively creating the future can by itself be an answer to prayer

God's Responsive Love

In the Old Testament, one of the most popular words to describe God's will is *righteousness*.

God's creation was seen as just and fair and wise—morally right. The Hebrew people believed the Law was given to them as an expression of God's care for them. The Law regulated and protected relationships in the community in ways intended to provide justice with order and peace. It provided a structure that created a healthy environment in which life could flourish. The Law was a gift of God's love. We understand today that there are things that God would have us do and things that we are not to do and that these limits are good for us and all creation.

The love of God has on occasion become "tough love." The Old Testament is full of stories about how God's people have experienced God's judgment in response to their disobedience. This judgment has been understood to be an expression of God's creating love. God sets limits for human behavior and exercises judgment to help us find the way as a parent exercises wise and just discipline as an expression of love for a child.

John Cobb talked with friends about God's responsive love:

> If we think of God as just and righteous, as Jews did in Paul's day, we may think also of God's wrath. There was much then for God to be wrathful about, and there is even more today.
>
> But Paul saw that Jesus revealed that God's judgment and righteousness are not wrath but love. That does

not mean that God intervenes to save humanity from the consequences of its acts, and today those consequences are profoundly frightening. But it does mean that God will not add divine punishment to those inevitable consequences. Instead, God is working in us and with us even now to ameliorate these consequences and bring about the best, or least destructive outcome that is still possible.[26]

God's love is unique. We see this most clearly in God's reaction to our human failings and disobedience. Christians have used the word *grace* in an attempt to distinguish God's love from all other forms of affection and attraction that we call love. God's love is unconditional. We do not deserve it. We cannot earn it. It is a gift.

We see God's responsive love most clearly in Christ. The life and teachings of Jesus, his sacrificial death, and his resurrection put a human face on God's grace. God sees our sin, our failures, and our weakness and does not stop loving us. God meets us where we are with forgiveness and a call to move on toward becoming the person God has created us to be.

One of the most beautiful pictures in Scripture of God's responsive love is the parable of the prodigal son (Luke 15:11-32). The father in the story runs to welcome home a son who has wasted all the father has given to him and then calls for an extravagant celebration because the son has seen the error of his ways and has come back to the family. The father receives the son in his present deteriorated condition and offers him new gifts of grace in a fresh set of possibilities for his future. The father did not force the son to stay at home in the first place, and neither did he make the son come home. The son exercised his free will, and the father responded with love.

The grace of God makes possible prayers of confession with the gift of forgiveness and new life.

Prayer as Openness _with_ God

What is the point in telling God anything if God already knows everything about you much better than you know yourself? Why is it necessary to share your needs and wants with God if all hearts are open and no secrets hidden? Why has openness *with* God been a constant part of the history of Christian prayer?

Telling God about your life and your concerns is more for you than for God. In prayer, you put on the table your joys, your gratitude, your hopes, your guilt, your needs, and your deepest concerns. You invite God's involvement. These things are no longer just your business. You open the door of your life to let God offer you the ideal possibilities that are God's gift of grace to you.

I once heard someone say, "I don't know what I think until I hear myself say it." There is value in expressing your feelings freely and openly in a safe setting so you can more completely know your own truth. Prayer can be that setting. God already knows, but in your telling, it becomes something the two of you are working on together. You are not weaving alone. Your prayer has provided God with an opening into your life, and that makes a difference in what God can offer you and do through you.

As "a rose is a rose is a rose," so prayer is prayer is prayer. But any rose fancier knows there are hybrid tea roses and climbing roses and miniature roses. With prayer there are threads of many colors and textures—prayers of praise, prayers of confession, prayers for one's own need and for the needs of others, prayers for guidance, prayers of dedication, listening prayer, meditation on Scripture, contemplation. You may pick up the thread of confession when your heart is heavy with guilt, share your feelings with God, express your repentance, and ask for forgiveness. You can accept the forgiveness, respond to God's leading about what you can do to make amends, and continue to weave with that burden lifted. You can weave the thread of praise into your design when you feel awe at the goodness of God. You can weave a thread of thanksgiving when you feel gratitude for God's gifts and unfailing grace. You can pick up the thread of petition when you need God's guidance or strength, share with God your needs, and let your weaving incorporate God's response.

Chapters 3 through 6 address in greater detail prayer as opening *with* God in these traditional ways.

The thread of prayer is indeed a two-way communication with God, with mutual listening and talking. It is also a mysterious linking of the human and the divine, an incomprehensible wonder, a miracle of miracles. And prayer warms one's soul before the glow of God.

PRAYER PROMPTS 3
The Thread of Prayer

I come to prayer seeking to come to my
senses in the presence of your holy love.

Centering

Be still and know that I am God.[27]
I'm goin' to pray when the Spirit says pray, and obey the Spirit of
the Lord.[28]

Praise

Eternal God, I adore you, whose name is love,
whose nature is compassion, whose presence is joy,
whose Word is truth, whose Spirit is goodness,
whose holiness is beauty, whose will is peace,
whose service is perfect freedom,
and in knowledge of whom stands my eternal life. [29]

I praise you for...

Confession

If I say that I have no sin, I deceive myself. If I confess my sins, you are faithful and just and will forgive my sins and give me a clean heart.[30] Trusting in this grace, I confess...

Forgive me and set me back on the path to the life you have created me to live.

If we claim that we're free of sin, we're only fooling ourselves. A claim like that is errant nonsense. On the other hand, if we admit our sins, God will forgive our sins and purge us of all wrong doing. [31]

Meditative Reading of Scripture

Petition

I pray for an awareness of your presence, inspiring, challenging, and giving me strength in these ways...

I am open to your guidance for setting priorities for my life, beginning today...

I pray for spiritual growth. As I grow in prayer, may I see you more clearly, love you more dearly, and follow you more nearly day by day...[32]

I pray for...

Intercession

I pray for those I find difficult to love. When I am worn out by them, irritated by their needs, impatient with their idiosyncrasies and limitations, give me grace to see below the surface into their hearts, to sympathize more deeply with their needs, to support what is lovely in them, and to know how to pray for them. I pray for…

I pray for peace. Guide all of your human children in the ways of mutual respect and commitment to serving the common good. I pray today for a place that needs peace…

I pray for those who are close to me and whose needs I observe on a regular basis. I share with you my concerns and hopes for them. May they receive the gifts of grace you offer to them.
I remember especially…

Thanksgiving

Eternal Spirit, your never-failing grace is the source of all hope and the lure that tugs me in the direction of all good things. Thank you for the goodness I do not deserve and cannot earn or repay. Today I am especially thankful for…

Dedication

Send me, Lord. Lead me, Lord. Fill me, Lord. Send me, Lord.[33]

Silence

Benediction

May the God of hope fill you with joy and peace through the power
of the Holy Spirit.

Scripture Passages for Meditative Reading or Group Study

Passages about the love of God:
> Psalm 103:1–5
> Psalm 103:8–18
> John 3:16–17
> Luke 15:11–32
> Romans 8:31–39
> Romans 5:1–5
> Psalm 69:13–18

CHAPTER 3

Asking Prayer

Ask, and it will be given you; search, and you will
find; knock, and the door will be opened for you.
Luke 11:9

The model prayer Jesus gave his disciples asked for things—
practical, ordinary things—like daily bread, guidance, and
deliverance from evil. Christians have been asking God for things
ever since. Much of what we do as we weave our lives involves
obtaining and using the necessities of life, deciding what to do
next, and avoiding danger. We talk to God about all of these
things, not only for ourselves but for each other.

The pronouns in the model prayer are plural—*our* instead of
my, *us* instead of *me*. This is a community prayer that includes
individuals and their unique needs but takes into consideration
the well-being of all. But the agenda of this prayer is the same for
private prayer for individuals.

The testimony of Christians across the centuries is that the
process of asking God is simple.

1. Trust in God's love.
2. Open your heart to share what is there.

3. Tell God what you want and need.
4. Listen for God's response.
5. Leave the prayer with God.

Trust in God's Love

As was said in the last chapter, God loves you and wills your unique set of ideal possibilities to become reality for you. God also loves all of creation and wills the ultimate good for all of it. The starting point for an asking prayer is trusting in God's love and good will for the one who prays and for the subjects of one's prayer.

I once belonged to a prayer group of five ministers who met once a month. We shared with each other in response to the question John Wesley posed to the early Methodists in England in the eighteenth century: "How goes it with your soul?" Group members took turns sharing about the major concerns of our lives (in a ten-minute summary). Then each of the others prayed for the one who had just shared. As my retirement date approached, I shared with the group my sense that soon my future would be a blank page. My husband had recently died, and I was planning to move from California to North Carolina to be near my family in the southeast. All of my previous involvements would be winding down, and I would be starting on what would come next. One of the ministers prayed in response, "Well, God, we are eagerly waiting to see what you are going to do with that blank page. We trust that you have plans and that you will make them known to Martha. We are interested to see what you are going to do and how you are going to do it." I did not know whether to laugh or cry. It was such a wonderful example of open trust. He didn't even ask. He just trusted that God's loving will would unfold as those days came. When I turned for that thread, it would be there. He was celebrating that faith with me and for me.

Trusting in God's loving will does not mean expecting that God will give us exactly what we ask for in the way we ask for it. Jesus expressed his feelings and his needs to God openly and honestly. He did this in the larger context of his ultimate trust in God. He subordinated his prayers to the will of God, which he believed would be an expression of divine love and would be better than he could pray. Jesus put his "your kingdom come, your will be done" petitions in his model prayer before the personal requests. He put his anguished prayer in the garden of Gethsemane in the context of his ultimate trust in God's good will. His life was on the line, but he prayed trustingly, "Let this cup pass from me... nevertheless, not my will but your will be done."

Jesus' prayers highlight an important distinction between Christian prayer and primitive magic. Prayer, for some people, is to ask and to expect the answer to be identical to the request. They see this as a complete and adequate definition of prayer. Prayer can become nothing more than a way of employing supernatural powers to get something you want that seems to be beyond your human to be beyond your human reach. Here are two humorous examples: In an interview, a coach was asked what he planned to do to prepare for a game in which the odds were against his team three to one. He answered, "Pray a lot." A minister made a hole-in-one on a golf course. His golfing partner exclaimed, "Don't tell me you haven't been praying!"

Christian petition differs from magic in one major way. The goal in Christian prayer is to communicate with God rather than to manipulate God. The individual's will is expressed so it can be harmonized with God's vision and purpose. We tell God what we think we and others want and need. But these petitions are set in the context of trust in and commitment to God's will.

Open Your Heart to Share What Is There

This part of asking prayer can be thought of in two steps: (1) identify the need, and (2) share your concern with God. God already knows everything, but the subject of your prayer needs to be put on the table.

Sometimes the need is not clear, and we may not know what we want. Jane Vennard describes how she felt when her mother was dying: "I was confused. One moment I would pray for her to be healed; the next that she would be released. I would pray that God would give her courage to go on. I would pray for her to let go. My heart was in turmoil, so my prayers were in turmoil."[34]

Prayers don't have to be in perfect form before they are offered. The starting place for prayer is where you are. Clarity about the need can come out of the dialogue of prayer.

Some people find that writing in a journal as if describing the need to God or as if sending an e-mail to God about the situation can help clarify the prayer request. Others simply focus their minds and hearts on their concerns, trusting that God perceives their thoughts and feelings and gets the picture.

The temptation is to leave the prayer with a description of the problem. But prayer is not just for complaining to God about how things are. Asking prayer involves turning your attention from what is to what you hope for and want. It is an opportunity for opening up to a new thing—what God wills for your weaving in this moment.

After a person shared in my ministers' prayer group, others would ask, "How can we pray for you?" The answer to the "What do you want?" question helped to focus feelings and a sense of need and gave the rest of us clear requests to share. Listening for and recognizing an answer is easier when the request is clear.

Tell God What You Want and Need

In Luke's gospel we see Jesus' clearest instruction on the subject of opening your heart freely and fully. "Ask, and it will be given to you; search, and you will find; knock, and the door will be opened to you" (Luke 11:9). This admonition follows the Lord's Prayer in Luke's gospel. Jesus is teaching here about prayer. Our asking, searching, and knocking are important in the process of receiving. If we do not assert our will in prayer, God may not be able to offer us the possibilities that would be available if we expressed our desires with strength.

Petitioning prayer begins with sharing how things are now and moves to the best possible outcome you can imagine. Asking involves following, "Here is how I see this situation," with, "This is my best judgment about or my hope for the future here."

The asking can be very simple, even in a formal liturgical prayer. One might say, "We remember the suffering people in this war-torn country, and we pray for an end of conflict and the return to peace."

Your best hopes can be expressed in words, either spoken aloud or silently in your thoughts. Creative visualization is sometimes helpful, especially for people who are more visual than verbal. You can visualize a person who is ill as well and whole again. You can see someone going through a challenging situation as having come through that time successfully. You can make these visualizations your prayer. One possibility for a situation when you don't know enough to pray specifically is to imagine the person for whom you are praying as surrounded by a warm and healing light that symbolizes the love and healing power of God.

Christian prayer is not pure passivity and receptivity. Jesus repeatedly commended assertiveness in prayer. Luke says that Jesus taught his disciples to "pray always and not to lose heart" (Luke 18:1). A Syrophonecian woman, through her tenacity, convinced Jesus to grant her request to free her daughter from a demon (Mark 7:25–30). Jesus affirmed the boldness of the woman with the issue of blood who reached out from the crowd to touch his robe in the belief she would be healed. Jesus said, "Daughter, your faith has made you well; go in peace" (Luke 8:43–48).

The experience of thinking as hopefully as you can also opens your mind to the creative possibilities that may be God's will. Prayer that stops with just reporting concerns and needs misses the opportunity of communing with God about what God would have happen.

A member of my congregation in my early ministry was hospitalized in an isolation unit. I could not visit her, but I could talk to her on the telephone. We had a good conversation, and as I prepared to hang up, I said, "I will be praying for you." "Oh no!" she responded in alarm. "Don't do that!" Startled, I asked the reason for her concern. "If you pray for me, you will just be thinking negative thoughts about all that is wrong with me and the scary possibilities here. You will be sending out negative vibes about me, and I don't want that!" I offered to pray for her by visualizing her well and happy and sharing a cup of tea in the late afternoon with her husband in their backyard Japanese garden. "Oh yes," she said. "Please do pray for me that way." A couple of months later, I joined her and her husband for tea in that garden. We smiled as we remembered the earlier prayer.

Sometimes focusing your attention on a prayer's desired outcome can help you to see ways to become part of the answer to your prayer. "If that is what is needed, then I can help in this way!"

People in groups, organizations, institutions, and problem situations are all appropriate subjects for intercession. The liturgical prayers of the church traditionally have included general prayers for the sick, the poor, the troubled, the lonely, victims of war, and other special circumstances of need. When we share in God's concern for the suffering in the world, our prayers reflect the spirit of the asking dimensions of the Lord's Prayer.

Asking prayers can be seen as making two kinds of impacts on the design of one's life tapestry. The first can be called a weaving prayer. This prayer is about an ongoing concern, and it may be part of a significant section of your life. The thread of this petition may appear over and over in your prayers, changing and growing as the situation evolves. You might pray on a regular basis for a special need in your life or in your family or in the world with the prayer becoming_shaped by the insights you receive in listening as well as by what happens. A second kind of asking prayer can be called a crisis prayer or an arrow prayer. A need is felt in a moment, but the crisis passes and you move on. The life impact may be intense but not long lasting. The thread appears once and not again.

A journal may be helpful in weaving prayers. You can express the concern in writing, telling it like it is without editing and including the facts and feelings as you know them. You can write your hopes and best wishes. You can use these prayers repeatedly, adding, subtracting, and editing as needed.

The crisis prayer is often a short prayer, usually in response to some circumstance or reminder. An ambulance sounds, and you send a prayer like an arrow shot from a bow for the person being carried in the ambulance and for those who provide care. The television presents breaking news of tragedy, and you interrupt your train of thought and activity to pray a short prayer for all involved. You face a difficult appointment, and you quickly ask for God's help in knowing what to do and how to do it.

My favorite example of an arrow prayer is from Allan Hunter. When he was about to meet someone, he used a prayer that was both for himself and for the other person: "Won't you, O God, express at least a little of your interest in this person through me right now?"[35]

You take God's love for you seriously and open a way for that love to enter your life when you ask God for what you need. You may miss what God wants to give you if you are totally absorbed in coping on your own or looking for what you need everywhere but from God. Prayer is one of the ways God's healing, saving work is done in each one of us and in the world. What you want and what you need are core parts of who you are. When you share this with God in prayer, you make this central part of your identity available for the gifts of grace God has for you.

Listen for God's Response

After you have communicated your understandings, feelings, and needs and expressed your best hopes, take time to listen. Wait expectantly to hear with your heart and mind, not your ears, to what God might give you in terms of guidance, support, courage, hope, love, and peace in response to your prayer.

A pastor friend, Rob Blackburn, remembers a special experience of listening prayer at a summer youth camp. He was a senior in high school and thinking about his future plans. He realized he was hearing the speakers at the camp as if they were speaking directly to him personally, so late in the week, he walked down the Meditation Path to a cross standing on the beach by a lake. He prayed a simple prayer, asking God for guidance and direction for his life. The prayer, he says, was nothing special. He did not hear a voice giving specific directions. But he says sometimes prayer goes where you are no longer saying words. His prayer became a visceral, heartfelt desire. And that is when an answer came. It was not audible, and at first it was a little bit disappointing. He had been hoping for a fortune cookie answer—a specific direction for the future. What he received was "a deep conviction that I was known, I was needed, I was loved, and I was in every way possible to share that love whatever I might be doing." Details did not seem to be important to God at that point. Looking back now, he realizes that God's will becomes known to us through the years in an ongoing relationship. We will get instructions and help along the way as we ask and listen.[36]

Again, listening and writing in a journal can help clarify the answer you receive. I sometimes write my understanding of the need and my best hopes for the situation and then review what I have written while listening to hear what God's response may be. The answer may be felt rather than heard, as with Rob's deep conviction.

We can expect that our petitions for ourselves and our intercessions for others may be changed as we listen in prayer.

God's answer may be that our wishes and desires will be clarified, purified, and matured. A prayer that begins as an honest but largely self-centered expression of need may become transformed into a wider-ranging request.

A weaving prayer itself may change several times in the process of being prayed before it can be answered in the context of God's broader vision. Start with honest sharing, expecting purification in the process.

One way prayer changes us is that in praying for others we open ourselves to God's love for all of creation. Listening to God's response to our prayers will inevitably draw us beyond our limited self-concern. Jesus taught his disciples to pray for their enemies. "Love your enemies, do good to those who hate you, bless those who curse you, pray for those who abuse you" (Luke 6:27–28). He demonstrated that kind of love from the cross. "Father, forgive them for they do not know what they are doing" (Luke 23:34). We can see people to whom we are not attracted or by whom we are threatened—our enemies—against the background of God's love for them. We can join with God in willing good things for them. Such intercession in the spirit of Christ has the power of creative transformation.

You may find new direction for your efforts and new insight into what you can do in listening to God's responses to your prayers. Your sensitivity may be enhanced and your motivation strengthened.

Sometimes praying is all you can do. While listening, you may find peace assuring you that God's creative and healing love is at work in ways that are beyond your understanding.

A later chapter in this book deals with the listening dimension of prayer in more detail.

Leave the Prayer with God

Finally, leave the prayer and move ahead. Trust that you have been heard and that God is actively "making all things new" and will answer in God's way in God's time.

In the movie *Amadeus*, the Viennese composer Solieri prays fervently as a young man, asking God to give him gifts to make the most beautiful music ever written. He promises in return to use the gifts to create music to glorify God. He offers God a deal: you do this for me, and I will do that for you. He becomes a respected professional musician. But then the brash, egotistical young Mozart arrives in Vienna. Mozart thoughtlessly offends Solieri, who is tortured by the younger man's musical genius. Solieri becomes furious with God and burns a crucifix in the fireplace. God had given the gifts Solieri prayed for to this arrogant young man! Feeling betrayed, Solieri plots to destroy one of the greatest musicians in history because God did not do what he asked in the way he asked it. He wants what he wants the way he wants it. His refusal to accept something different blocks him from hearing what God is calling him to do with the gifts he has been given.

We join our psychic energy, our hearts, to the love of God in active goodwill when we pray for others. How this works remains a mystery. Archbishop William Temple has been quoted as saying, "When I pray, coincidences happen; when I don't, they don't!"

The particular thing for which you pray may not happen just the way you prayed for it, but there will be an answer for you. The answer can be expected to be consistent with God's overall creative and redemptive purposes. The answer may be something even better than the thing for which you prayed. God's answer may be even better than you could have imagined. The answer may not be a change of circumstances but the resources for coping with circumstances. The answer may not be outer change but inner change. God's answer may be part of an ongoing process of helping the one who prays to grow spiritually in a way that could not happen by the simple granting of the request as expressed. The answer may stretch you to think about your situation in a new way or to see things from a more mature or healthy perspective. It may provide a new experience of comfort or hope or strength that will deepen your faith. It may be a nudge to reach out in a helpful way you have not tried before. The answer may be the healing of a deep wound that is causing the superficial pain about which you have prayed. The answer may come from the south when you are looking to the north, from the right when you are looking to the left.

Prayers for healing raise many questions if they are not answered as asked. Especially difficult are prayers that seem to be unanswered because the one for whom you are praying dies. But death is a part of God's plan for all of us. Prayer in faith trusts that even in death those about whom we pray are in God's care, and we can receive even that answer in trust and in hope that goes beyond this life.

What are some responses of faith when the answer to prayer is not clear?

- Pray about the prayer itself, and ask God to show you if you "ask wrongly" (James 4:3). The prayer may need to be transformed from selfish purposes to a genuine desire to share in the will of God. Praying about the prayer may give God an opportunity to help you by maturing the prayer so it can be answered in the context of the will of God.

- Pray persistently the same prayer. The time may not be right for the answer now. God is not your servant; you are God's servant. In answer to persistent praying, God may show you over time ways you can be active in answering the prayer yourself. And the prayer will be answered in God's way in God's time.

- Acknowledge that sometimes the power of prayer is blocked by the resistance of other people. Jesus cared about the people of his hometown, Nazareth. But even Jesus "could do no deed of power there... He was amazed at their unbelief" (Mark 6:1–6). God chooses to be limited by human free will. We should not try to control other people against their will through prayer.

- Leave the prayers in God's care. God's ways are beyond our understanding. In prayer there is mystery that is beyond our comprehension. We have to do our best and leave the rest to God.

PRAYER PROMPTS 4
Asking Prayer

I come to prayer eager to be enabled to
look at the future with serene confidence.

Centering

Ask, and it will be given you; search, and you will find; knock, and
the door will be opened for you.[37]

Those who wait for the Lord shall renew their strength, they shall
mount up with wings like eagles, they shall run and not be weary,
they shall walk and not faint.[38]

Praise

I sing the goodness of the Lord, who filled the earth with food,
who formed the creatures thru the Word, and then pronounced
them good.
Lord, how thy wonders are displayed, wher-e'er I turn my eye,
If I survey the ground I tread, or gaze upon the sky.[39]

I praise you for…

Confession

O God, you have set forth the way of life in your beloved Son. I confess with shame my slowness to learn of him, my reluctance to follow him. You have spoken and called, and I have not paid attention. Your beauty has shown forth and I have been blind. You have stretched out your hands to me through other people, and I have passed by. I have taken great benefits with little thanks. I have been unworthy of your changeless love. Hear my confession, and forgive me of these and all my sins…[40]

Hear the good news: In the name of Jesus Christ, you are forgiven.

Meditative Reading of Scripture

Petition

I bring to you the deepest needs of my life, as I understand them, asking for gifts of your grace in response to these needs as you know them. I pray for…

Help me to purge from my life prejudice against those who are different from me, especially in this situation. I pray for…

O Lord, my God, you are always more ready to give your good gifts to me than I am to ask for them. You are willing to give me more than I deserve. Help me to joyfully receive what you would give. I pray for…[41]

Intercession

I pray for those who grieve over loss. Protect them from bitterness and despair, and bring them through to peace and new hope. I remember especially…

I pray for our physical environment. Teach us to live in harmony with the rest of your creation, to use its resources wisely, and as far as possible to repair the damage we have done. I pray for...

I pray for those suffer with health problems. I pray for the best use of human resources for healing and for the release of the body's forces for recuperation and repair. I pray for...

I pray for...

Thanksgiving

For the harvests of the Spirit, thanks be to God;
for the good we all inherit, thanks be to God;
for the wonders that surround us, for the truths that still confound us,
most of all, that love has found us, thanks be to God.[42]
I thank you for...

Dedication

Thou who art over us,
Thou who art one of us,
Thou who art
Also within us,
Give me a pure heart that I might see thee;
A humble heart, that I may hear thee;
A heart of love, that I may serve thee;
A heart of faith, that I may abide in thee.[43]

Silence

Benediction

Glory to God, whose power, working in us, can do infinitely more than we can ask or imagine.[44]

Scripture Passages for Meditative Reading or for Group Study

Passages about prayers of petition and intercession:
> Matthew 7:7–11
> Luke 8:42b–48
> Matthew 6:5–7
> Matthew 6:11–13
> Luke 18:1–8
> Colossians 1:9–12
> Ephesians 3:14–19

CHAPTER 4

Praying about the Past

O give thanks to the Lord, for he is good;
for his steadfast love endures forever.
1 Chronicles 16:34 and Psalm 106:1

All have sinned and fall short of the glory of
God; they are now justified by his grace as a gift,
through the redemption that is in Christ Jesus.
Romans 3:23–24

A knitter can catch a mistake or decide to change a pattern while knitting, pull out the needles, unravel some stitches, and do it over. A writer who uses a computer has several options: the backspace key, the delete key, the refresh key, or just inserting new information in the original text. But weaving your life does not offer the chance for a redo of the past. Each moment becomes permanent history as it happens.

But the fact that the past is unchangeable does not mean Christians do not pray about the past. In fact, praying about the past plays an important role in Christian spirituality. The life weaving one has already done may be finished, but the impact of the past on the future can be shaped by prayer. Two important dimensions of Christian prayer focus on the past: thanksgiving and confession.

Giving thanks to God for the blessings of the past and confessing to God the mistakes of the past open the way for God's grace to bring amazing healing and hope into the design of the current day.

Both ways of praying have roots in the ancient records in the Bible of the worship of our ancestors. For thousands of years of our faith history, people have been saying to God both, "Thank you for what has been" and "I regret something that I have done or left undone." Both are like the "unfinished business" item on the agenda at a committee meeting. Something in the past needs to be completed in the process of moving into the future. Prayer offers the opportunity to finish the job and to affect the impact of what has been on what will be.

Thanksgiving

A life tapestry that includes many threads of gratitude will be a thing of beauty. One of the liturgical prayers of the church is in the order for Holy Communion, and is called The Great Thanksgiving. Before worshippers receive the bread and cup, they pray, "It is a right, and a good and joyful thing, always and everywhere to give thanks to you, Father Almighty, creator of heaven and earth." Thanksgiving that is "always and everywhere" is a lifestyle—not just woven in occasionally when something especially nice happens. A lifestyle of gratitude is a good and joyful thing. When we take time to reflect on all of the good things God has provided for us and to say thank you, the world is brighter and our hearts are lighter. Thanksgiving brightens the tapestry of your life. And more importantly, your relationship with God is strengthened.

My husband and I were traveling by ourselves one Thanksgiving Day. We retired to our hotel room after our big dinner and decided to take turns telling each other about things for which we were thankful. We stopped two hours later, not because we were finished but because we were tired. This conversation was not formal prayer. However, we were expressing gratitude to God by remembering the blessings and speaking them because we were both clear about the source. I remember that as perhaps my best-ever Thanksgiving. The glow of gratitude lasted for several days.

It is possible to identify and give thanks for God's gifts even in the most difficult situations. Someone suggested to me once, when I was going through an extremely challenging time, that at the end of each day I ask myself the question, "Where have I seen the face of grace today?" I understood grace as the unlimited, unconditional love of God that we cannot deserve or earn and that is ours to trust throughout our lives. I kept a journal on that subject through those painful days. Every day people and events and amazing little shafts of light in my own spirit showed me the presence of God's grace with me. Expressing gratitude for this daily gift of the face of grace transformed that time for me and made it bearable. I had fresh insight into the spiritual wisdom of Paul's admonition to the church in Thessalonica: "Rejoice always, pray without ceasing, give thanks in all circumstances, for this is the will of God in Christ Jesus for you" (1 Thessalonians 5:16).

Thanksgiving serves to develop inner strength and hope. The expectation of God's future goodness is enhanced as God's past goodness is reviewed. You can expect that God will continue to do the same in the future if God has done all of these good things for you in the past. Our love for God grows when we take time to acknowledge what God has provided for us.

It has been said that a thankful person tastes joy twice—once when it happens and again when gratitude is expressed to God for the joy.

A good place to begin to learn to pray is saying thank you to God. Children often learn to pray thanksgiving prayers first and can do this with impressive imagination. You can express gratitude to God when called on to pray aloud in a group. Thanksgiving is always appropriate.

Confession

The gift of God's forgiveness was a major source of joyful gratitude for our ancestors in faith. The ancient believers trusted that the God who is present with us in every moment—who always knows what we have done and what we have left undone—has already forgiven us even before we confess. In forgiveness they experienced healing and new life, and they were grateful.

The psalmist mixes thanks for forgiveness with praise in a prayer of gratitude:

> Bless the Lord, O my soul, and all that is within me bless his holy name. Bless the Lord, O my soul, and do not forget all his benefits—who forgives all of your iniquity, who heals all of your diseases, who redeems your life from the Pit, who crowns you with steadfast love and mercy, who satisfies you with good as long as you live so that your youth is renewed like an eagle... The Lord is merciful and gracious, slow to anger and abounding in steadfast love... He does not deal with us according to our sins, nor repay us according to our iniquities. For as the heavens are high above the earth, so great is his steadfast love toward those who fear him; as far as the east is from the west, so far he removes our transgression from us (Psalm 103:1–5, 8, 10–12).

And Paul writes to Timothy:

> I am grateful to Christ Jesus our Lord, who has strengthened me, because he judged me faithful and appointed me to his service, even though I was formerly a blasphemer, a persecutor, and a man of violence. But I received mercy because I had acted ignorantly in unbelief, and the grace of our Lord

overflowed for me with the faith and love that are
in Christ Jesus (1 Timothy 1:12–14).

Why do we hear in Scripture so much gratitude for forgiveness?

Guilt about the past can be very destructive to us and to our ability to weave the kind of future toward which God is calling us. Life can be crippled by the burden of regret. Guilt can limit the possibilities God can offer to us when our consciousness is preoccupied with problems from the past that remain unresolved. Forgiveness can bring healing to us and to the world.

The psalmist gives a vivid picture of the price of guilt in the human spirit and the release that comes with forgiveness.

> Happy are those whose transgression is forgiven, whose sin is covered.
> Happy are those to whom the Lord imputes no iniquity, and in whose spirit is no deceit.
> While I kept silence, my body wasted away through my groaning all day long.
> For day and night your hand was heavy upon me; my strength was dried up as by the heat of summer.
> Then I acknowledged my sin to you, and I did not hide my iniquity;
> I said, "I will confess my transgression to the Lord," and you forgave the guilt of my sin. (Psalm 32:1–5)

Eugene Peterson, in his book *The Message*, paraphrases this passage:

> Count yourself lucky, how happy you must be -
> you get a fresh start, your slate's wiped clean.
> Count yourself lucky—God holds nothing against
> you and you're holding nothing back from him.

When I kept it all inside, my bones turned to
powder, my words became daylong groans.
The pressure never let up; all the juices of my life
dried up.
Then I let it all out; I said, "I'll make a clean breast
of my failures to God."
Suddenly the pressure was gone- my guilt dissolved,
my sin disappeared.

Forgiveness makes possible a fresh new future. Forgiveness opens the way for the call of God to sound clearly in your heart.

In Matthew's gospel (Matthew 3:2), John the Baptist preaches, "Repent, for the kingdom of heaven has come near." Something better is available, he is saying. Turn from what has been to what can be. Confession and repentance are future-oriented experiences, involving liberation from the regrets of the past to be able to take advantage of a hopeful future.

Confession is for all of us. Mother Teresa of Calcutta, perhaps one of the most Christ like figures of the twentieth century, went often to confession. A television interviewer, aware that Mother Teresa would probably be canonized as a saint by the church after her death, asked why she felt the need to confess. "I am a human being and a sinner," she responded, "so I need to go to confession regularly."

We all have regrets. We misuse our free will as human beings to make choices that alienate us from God, each other, and ourselves. We damage and destroy in ways large and small. We may not have bad intentions, but in a moment of carelessness or thoughtlessness or distraction by other interests, we do harm. We may slide into bad habits over time. We may absorb destructive attitudes and habits from our environment. We may be deluded into bad practices. We fail to be who God has created us to be. We wish for a way to make up for what we have done or to go back to fill in the blank left by things we did not do that we ought to have done. Our hearts can be heavy with regret.

People have tried many forms of escape from the pain of guilt when they have been unable to do anything about past mistakes. Painful memories can be tenacious, and efforts to escape don't work very well.

God's forgiveness in response to our confession provides the key to liberation and a new start. God is more interested in what we can become than in what we used to be. The Christian confession/repentance/forgiveness experience includes these traditional components:

1. **Confess.** God knows more about what you did or didn't do than you know. God is not in denial about your limitations, failures, mistakes, and inadequacies. God knows the growing edges of your Christian discipleship— the places where you just aren't there yet. God knows the ideal possibilities for you and how far you are from living into them. Your confession will be no surprise to God. Telling God about all of this is not the point. The point in confession is getting honest with yourself. This can be difficult and painful, but in the context of God's grace, focusing clearly on the ways in which you have failed to live up to God's will for you can be possible. You can leave the cave of denial and come out into the sunlight of the truth. You can separate the person from the sin and repent, trusting in God's unconditional love for you. Receiving forgiveness begins with admitting, confessing, and coming clean with both God and yourself.

2. **Repent.** Repentance is a profound version of "I'm sorry" combined with "and I won't do it again." Repentance for a pattern of behavior or an ongoing habit includes the intention to turn away from what is confessed and to aim in

a different direction. In the life-weaving image, one would intend to drop the thread confessed from future weaving.

3. **Receive forgiveness.** God's forgiveness is ready when your confession is made. God's responsive love works with our mistakes to see what can be done with what has been done.

   Prayers of confession, like asking prayers, can be weaving prayers that reoccur regularly in your weaving. Confession is not something you do once, but something that is part of the regular routine. Confession of a regret may need to be made several times while you get ready to let go of your guilt and accept God's grace. God's forgiveness is immediate when you ask for it. The acceptance of that forgiveness and the freedom to move on may take longer. Sometimes it is harder to forgive yourself than it is to understand that God has forgiven you.

4. **Make amends.** One of the most painful parts of regret about the past is the thought, *I can't do anything about it now.* But there may be things you can do that can mend the damage or heal the wounds.

5. **Ask for guidance in doing better.** Openness with God in confession can lead into openness to hear God's guidance and to find God's strength to provide power to improve.

The God who forgives is also the God who works with you to grow from the person you have been into the person you are called to be. The full gift of forgiveness calls forth the joyful prayer of gratitude when that happens.

Henry Ward Beecher, a notable American preacher of the nineteenth century, talked about the "nobility of confession." He said that although we often think of confession as humbling, even degrading, there is nothing more noble than recognizing a wrong, feeling and expressing sorrow for it, and renouncing it. You "breathe the very breath of heaven" when you have been honest with God, yourself, and each other by confessing your sins.

God responds to prayers about the past by building on them for the future God offers.

PRAYER PROMPTS 5
Praying about the Past

I come to prayer eager to be reminded
that my frailty does not matter.

Centering

O give thanks to the Lord, for he is good; for his steadfast love
endures forever.[45]

Send out your light and your truth, O God; let them lead me.[46]

Praise

My soul praises you, O God.
With all my being, I praise your holy name!
I will not forget all your benefits.
You fill my life with good things.
You judge in favor of the oppressed.
You do not punish us as we deserve.
Your goodness endures to all generations.
My soul praises you, O God.[47]
I praise you today for…

Confession

I confess to you, all-knowing God, that I am not the person I like others to think I am. I am afraid to admit, even to myself, what lies at the depths of my soul. But I cannot hide my true self from you. You know me as I am, and yet you love me. Teach me to respect myself as I am and to put my trust in your guiding power. Raise me out of the paralysis of guilt into the freedom and energy of a forgiven person. Restore me according to your promises in Christ Jesus. Grant that I may live to the glory of your holy name.[48] I confess...

Forgive my sins, O God. Do not remember my wrongs any more. Write your will upon my heart, and preserve me among your people.

Meditative Reading of Scripture

Petition

Save me from the worship of idols—money, success, power, popularity, another person...

I pray for guidance in dealing with my limitations. Help me to be patient with frustration and disappointment and wise about managing what I have. I pray especially for...

Help me to reach out hands of compassion. Guide me in assisting my brothers and sisters, especially with the burden carried by...

I pray for...

Intercession

I pray for those who suffer. May they receive from you healing, courage, comfort, and hope. I pray for...

I pray for those who take stands against injustice and protest things that damage human welfare. May they feel the empowering presence of your Spirit and find joy in their work. I remember today...

I pray for my family. Teach us to weave those fragile threads of gentle love that eventually combine to create a cable of trust and affection, binding us together. I pray today especially for...

I pray for...

Thanksgiving

O Lord, creator and giver of all good things, I thank you for the gift of life, for all of your creation, for your guidance in every moment of every day. I thank you for friends and for duties, for happy memories and hope for the future, for joys that brighten the days and for challenges that teach me to trust you. Give me wisdom to use well all of your gifts.[49]

I thank you for...

Dedication

O Christ, my only Savior, I pray that because you dwell in me, I may live with the light of your hope in my eyes and with your faith and love in my heart...[50]
I will...

Silence

Benediction

The grace of the Lord Jesus Christ be with your spirit.[51]

Scripture Passages for Meditative Reading or Group Study

Passages about thanksgiving and confession:

Psalm 32:1–5
Ephesians 5:15–20
Psalm 105:1–5
Psalm 51:1–17
Romans 7:14—8:2
Romans 3:21–26
1 Timothy 1:12–17

CHAPTER 5

Prayer As Listening

Speak Lord, for your servant is listening.
1 Samuel 3:9

Prayer as human monologue misses the best part—what God has to say to you. The major impact of prayer on the design of your life tapestry will come not so much from what you express in your side of the flow of communication as from what God gives to you when you listen.

God Speaks

The Bible frequently pictures God as speaking. In the creation story in Genesis 1, everything happened as a result of God's spoken word. "Let there be..." God said. And there was! God continued speaking and more things happened. Adam and Eve heard God's voice in the garden of Eden giving them the rules. They disobeyed and were in trouble. God warned Noah about the coming flood. He built a boat while his neighbors, who had not heard the warning, laughed. The Exodus story reports that "the Lord used to speak to Moses face to face, as one speaks to a friend" (Exodus 33:11). God talked Moses through the liberation of the Hebrew people from slavery in Egypt. God gave Moses the guidelines for healthy human communities in words carved on stone tablets (the Ten Commandments). God guided Moses in getting the people through the desert and ready to go into the Promised Land.

God's "speaking" in the biblical story is not always in words. Daniel interpreted God's messages that had come in the dreams of the king, and he saved his people. The Holy Spirit descended on Jesus at his baptism in the form of a dove. A voice "comes from heaven" saying, "You are my Son, the Beloved; with you I am well pleased" (Mark 1:11). With this baptism, the ministry of Jesus began. In the last week of his life, Peter was reminded he had betrayed Jesus when he heard the crow of a rooster. In the first days of the early church, Saul was knocked down by a "light from heaven" and heard a voice (Acts: 9:3-4). He instantly converted from persecuting Christians to organizing Christians into churches across the region and writing letters that now form a large portion of our New Testament.

The Scriptures provide abundant testimony from our faith history that God does communicate and that people have heard and trusted and received the messages. Life-changing, sometimes history-changing, messages came. Tapestries were transformed. God's work was done.

Church history is also replete with stories of God speaking and people hearing. Methodists hold dear the story of the founder of Methodism going unwillingly to a small chapel in London on May 24, 1738. John Wesley was steeped in Scripture and regularly practiced the habits of holy living that he had been taught in his remarkable family. But that night he heard Martin Luther's words read from his preface to the book of Romans about salvation through faith. Wesley later recorded in his journal that he felt his heart strangely warmed. He heard God speak to him at a deeper level of his being than ever before and in a powerful way. He was transformed by this experience into a new man with a new faith. Crowds gathered across England for decades to hear him preach this faith from that warmed heart. God spoke, and the Methodist movement was born.

People are still hearing from God, and lives are affected by the messages. God's messages continue to come in many forms. God does not have to use words heard through our ears but can speak directly to our minds and our spirits. Sometimes an answer to prayer is just there, clear as crystal, and you recognize it for what it is. It is as if words have been spoken. Sometimes you can recognize an answer to prayer in retrospect. You can look back and see how a prayer has been answered without you seeing what was happening. Sometimes a prayer is answered with a persistent nudge to do something. God's voice may be heard when a new idea or perspective lights up the mind or when a clear conviction emerges accompanied by the kind of peace and joy that only God can give.

An ancient way to recognize God's voice is to trust that God will provide feelings of consolation when you are on the right path and feelings of desolation when you are off-track. God's voice has been identified as the source when fresh courage, calm, or hope emerges, when a soul is strengthened, or when a temptation diminishes or is conquered. God's voice has been heard when problems untangle and tensions clear following prayer. God is sending messages all the time, and many may be impulses we do not notice consciously but that encourage us to make the best response at the moment.

How Do We Know What We Are Hearing Is from God?

Christians differ on the answer to this question. I think we agree that what God says will always be consistent with God's nature and God's loving purposes for all creation.

Some would say that finding a scriptural basis for what you think you have heard is essential. I have seen Scripture so contorted to prove someone's defense of a position that proof-texting alone does not work for me. I have heard days set as "the end time" and defenses for slavery based on Scripture alone. I have heard people cite a specific passage of Scripture as authority for saying "God told me to do this," attributing to God things most Christians would consider contrary to God's will.

There is tremendous power in the claim that one is being directed by God. Power is always vulnerable to abuse. The power of this claim has been widely and notoriously misused.

A safer test for a perceived answer to prayer is to test it against the whole of Scripture to see if it is consistent with what we know from the totality of the story of good news found there. Specific passages may give focus, but they are best viewed in the context of the full narrative.

I hesitate to write about receiving messages from God because of the disastrous history of people who have done destructive, wasteful things they claim that God told them to do. Hearing messages from God does not have a very good reputation in the public mind. But then I reflect that sinful human beings abuse all of God's good gifts. Our ancestors believed human beings from our earliest history were having trouble dealing with God's messages, so the creation story pictures Adam and Eve responding to a clear message from God by choosing almost immediately to listen instead to the snake.

This abuse does not negate the innate goodness of these gifts or the grace they provide in every moment of every day. God has been calling all of creation from the beginning from what it is to what it can be. And people have been and still are listening with positive results.

The test of fruitfulness is another test that can be applied to a deep conviction you are hearing a message from God. "If I act on this as God's call to me, does my action bear fruit that reflects God's will in the world?"

The United Methodist system for ordaining ministers includes this test. Candidates are asked if they feel a deep conviction of a call to the ministry from God. If the answer is yes, the next step is to get references and recommendations from a local church. Do others who know this person well and have observed his or her practice of the Christian life see this deep conviction as truly a call from God? If the answer is again yes, the candidate may be ordained on a probationary basis, and the call is tested in a church assignment. Only after observing the fruit of this person's practice of ministry does the church confer ordination as a sign of confirming the call to ministry.

As a parish minister, I experienced this same test of fruitfulness over the decision to build a new sanctuary for the congregation. Several people expressed in prayerful planning sessions a deep conviction that the time was right to complete this dream of many years. We were in a recession, and I was uneasy. We decided to trust that this was indeed God's call to us in this moment. I watched carefully for signs of fruitfulness as we moved ahead. We experienced wonderful spiritual growth together as we tackled this project in faith and watched it happen before our eyes. The new sanctuary has been a blessing to the church and the community from day one. We agree in retrospect that this clearly was the will of God for us in that moment.

We Listen

Listening is an inadequate word for the experience of receiving messages from God, but it is the best word we have. Listening is at least an active word and communicates intentional openness to receive a message.

God's speaking is not dependent on our listening. In the biblical stories cited earlier, God sometimes caught people by surprise and said unexpected things on subjects not even on the mind of the person addressed. Sometimes people were startled or stunned. But they were not uncertain about the source of the message. This can still happen.

You can also actively listen for God's individually tailored messages on subjects that *are* on your mind. These messages are more readily available than information on the Internet.

Knowing what God has in mind for you as a person of faith is the most valuable information there is.

What Can Help You to Hear?

1. *Wanting to hear from God*

Active listening for answers to prayers may come from the heart in the form of deep yearning to know God's will for the weaving you are doing now. The psalmist expresses this yearning for God. "As a deer longs for a stream of cool water, so I long for you, O God" (Psalm 40:1), he says in one psalm. In another he says, "Your word is a lamp to guide me and a light for my path" (Psalm 119:105). The Lord's Prayer asks that God's will be done before asking anything else.

Rick Warren, pastor of Saddleback Church in California, makes a distinction between "nice" and "necessary" in listening prayer. You will not hear God's answers to your prayers, he says, if you are listening just because it would be nice to know—to have God's will as an option. When you listen to hear and to do, when God's call is necessary for you to know before you move forward, you can hear. A listening prayer tells God yes in advance. It communicates, "I know that I can trust you to know better than I know. I want to do what you want me to do."[52]

Moses taught the Hebrew people about the need for an all-or-nothing approach to asking God. He said, "You will find God if you search after him with all your heart and soul" (Deuteronomy 4:29).

2. *Paying attention*

Careful listening is a challenge in the twenty-first century. Life can be complex and noisy. Messages bombard us from all directions. We carry with us electronic devices full of messages, and we fill every spare minute with receiving and sending information. Change is occurring at an accelerating rate. As soon as we have learned how to do something, we hear that it has been superseded by a new way. We have to master the innovation or be left behind. Our minds are continually challenged and busy.

Can you imagine how much quieter and simpler life was in

first-century Galilee? Yet Jesus felt the need to go away from his disciples to a quiet place to pray (Luke 5:16). He instructed his disciples, "When you pray, go to your room, close the door, and pray to your Father, who is unseen" (Matthew 6:6).

Susannah Wesley, a parish priest's wife in eighteenth-century England and the mother of nineteen children, is said to have used her apron as a sign to her family that she was listening to God and was not to be disturbed. She would sit down in a chair and pull her apron over her head. Any child who disturbed her during this time could be in serious trouble. The children apparently learned the necessity of focused attention in prayer from their mother. One son, John, was the founder of the Methodist movement. Another son, Charles, wrote hymns that are still sung in Christian worship around the world more than two hundred years later.[53]

Paying attention is a matter of focus. The psalmist put it succinctly: "Be still and know that I am God" (Psalm 46:10). Tune out the distractions around you, and turn your attention to a quiet center within.

The practice of centering is drawing your attention into a focus so the mind can move to the heart. Attention to breathing can help you to grow quiet. Taking a few deep, slow breaths can make deep relaxation possible. Fill your lungs with air. Observe the gentle breathing in of cool air through the nostrils and into the lungs and then the breathing out of warm air. Awareness of this natural rhythm in your body prepares the mind for the inner communion of prayer. Transition to prayer can be made by remembering that God is like the air you breathe, present in this moment both within you and beyond you.

In the quiet, you can begin by becoming aware of the life that is in you, the gift of the Creator who is also present in this moment. Then you can move on to your agenda with God and God's agenda with you.

Focusing your attention with this centering process initially may take a few minutes. Centering can be done more quickly and easily with practice

A friend told me about his experience listening to a famous organist getting ready for a concert on the organ of his church. He slipped quietly into the back of the sanctuary on the morning of the concert, expecting to hear parts of the brilliant music scheduled for the evening. Instead, he heard her playing one note at a time and a series of notes over and over. Later he asked her about this. "I was working on muscle memory," she told him. "That part of the piece is so fast that my brain has to depend on my muscles to remember it." With practice, the process of centering for prayer can become part of your spiritual memory so you can center quickly. Your spirit knows the way because it goes there often.

Hearing the answer may be startlingly instantaneous, or it may take time. On a few occasions, I have barely finished posing the question before the answer is there. From the time of focused attention, you can take with you the openness to hear. If you wait expectantly, the message that is there will become clear in time.

3. Listening for God's response to your prayers

Listening prayer can be part of other forms of traditional Christian prayer. When you are already weaving one of the threads of prayer into your tapestry, listening time may be just waiting to hear God's response

A prayer of confession may lead you to ask God to show you where you are not living as God would have you to live. You may gain insight about how you can make reparations for damage done. Confession also may end in a time of listening to receive God's forgiveness. A prayer of petition or intercession may include asking for guidance on what role you can play in answering the prayer. A silent time of listening may produce insights not before perceived. Prayer about how to pray in a particular situation, followed by a time of listening, may open up new directions.

I find it helpful to think about what God might want to have happen by trying to see the larger picture from God's point of view—the view of love and compassion for everyone and everything involved. This means listening for the call of God in this moment in time and especially for that call to me. The answer is often amazing, and I am left wondering, "Why did I not see that or think of that?"

4. Asking a question and listening for the answer

If you are not already weaving a thread of prayer, you may want to ask a specific question for which you want an answer. If you journal, you may want to record the question, and that will help you recognize the answer.

Special Kinds of Listening Prayer

Praying the Scriptures

Reading Scripture is a very popular way to listen to God. Dietrich Bonhoeffer wrote in *Life Together*, "The most promising method of prayer is to allow oneself to be guided by the word of the Scriptures, to pray on the basis of a word of Scripture. In this way, we shall not become victims of our own emptiness."[54]

In praying the Scripture, you approach the text by listening for the word of God in a personal way. You put yourself into the text, looking for connections between your personal story and God's story. Sermons in congregational worship and printed devotional resources often assist us in making the connection between Scripture and our daily life.

The message of the passage is encountered not by the head but by the heart in praying the Scripture. The Word is connected directly to your life.

Reuben Job has shared questions to ask when "bowing in the presence of the Word in Scripture": God, what are you saying to me? What is your word in this passage for me? What are you saying about my life? What am I to be/become? What are you calling me to do?[55]

Lectio Divina

The Benedictine order in the Roman Catholic Church has an ancient tradition of listening prayer that has been instructive to many contemporary Christians. This is the pattern of *lectio divina* (pronounced lex-ee-oh dih-vee-nuh) or divine reading, a structure of four movements for prayerful reading of Scripture. These movements are:

> *Lectio:* READ the material as if receiving food for life. Read as if listening to the One who is behind the words. Read twice, once for general overview of the passage and once more slowly to see if any word or phrase or sentence attracts your attention as if inviting exploration.
>
> *Meditatio:* REFLECT on the passage as if chewing on the words and tasting God's gift in them. Listen to hear what message God may have for you today.
>
> *Oratio:* RESPOND to God in light of what you hear. Share with God what you most need to share.
>
> *Contemplatio:* REST in the presence of God. Be quiet with the thoughts of what you have heard, and open yourself to any new insights or inspirations that may come.

The best Scripture passages for *lectio divina* are brief and active, with concrete images.

Labyrinth

Walking the labyrinth is an ancient prayer practice for listening for answers to specific questions. The labyrinth is being rediscovered in contemporary Christianity. The most famous Christian labyrinth was inlaid in the floor of the cathedral at Chartres, France, during the thirteenth century. Pilgrims have come from all over the world to pray as they walk the path of this labyrinth. In the eleventh and twelfth centuries, the church instructed good Christians to make at least one pilgrimage to the Holy Land in their lifetimes. Because travel to the Holy Land was very expensive and dangerous, labyrinths were laid out in six different cathedrals in Europe so people could make a symbolic journey. Walking the labyrinth became over time a symbol for the spiritual journey and an aid to prayer.

The labyrinth looks like a circular maze, usually about forty-two feet in diameter. A maze is designed to confuse, with dead ends along the path and a devious design. But the labyrinth's design guides the walker on his or her way. A single narrow path opens from the outside of the circle and winds its way into an open space at the middle of the circle. The walker is free to trust the path and to be absorbed in prayer while simply putting one foot in front of the other.

One of the traditions for walking the labyrinth is a three-step process. In the first stage, the time walking slowly toward the center of the labyrinth, the walker reflects on the question: "What needs to be let go in my life?" This is a time of centering and quieting, becoming open and receptive. In the second stage, one stands in the center of the labyrinth and spends time in receptive meditation listening. In the third stage, walking slowly out from the center, the walker responds with willingness to incorporate what has been received into his or her life and to draw on the power to do that. The question for the walk out of the labyrinth is sometimes described as, "What do I need to add to my life?"

The discipline of slowly walking a trusted path engages the whole person in attentive listening.

Listening prayer can be free-standing, with no prior questions or prayers involved. You can simply spend time in open listening to what God might be saying to you.

It can be argued that listening prayer is what we need most because our souls are hungry for God.

PRAYER PROMPTS 6
Prayer as Listening

I come to prayer eager to realize that I am infinitely loved.

Centering

Worship God in spirit and truth, for this is what God wants.[56]

Speak, Lord, for your servant is listening.[57]

Praise

I saw the Lord always before me, for he is at my right hand so that I will not be shaken; therefore my heart was glad and my tongue rejoiced; moreover my flesh will live in hope. You have made known to me the ways of life; you will make me full of gladness with your presence.[58]

I praise you for...

Confession

Holy and awesome God, I stand in your presence filled with regret for my many sins and failings. Though there is greatness in me and a deep longing for goodness, I have often denied my better self and refused to hear your voice calling me to rise to the full height of my humanity. For there is weakness in me as well as strength.

At times I choose to walk in darkness, my vision obscured. I do not care to look within, and I am unwilling to look beyond at those who need my help. O God, I am too weak to walk unaided. Be with me as a strong and wise friend, and teach me to walk by the light of your truth.

I confess…

The Lord God is merciful and gracious, endlessly patient, loving and true, forgiving and granting pardon.[59]

Meditative Reading of Scripture

Petition

I pray for freedom from fear and anxiety. Help me to find peace and to know what to do about the things that frighten me, especially…

Make me whole with the gift of your healing touch where I need it today…

I pray for the expansion of my love by the infusion of your love into my heart. Purge me of hatred and vengefulness with the power of your love. I pray for new resources for loving in this situation…

I pray for…

Intercession

I pray for those who have lost hope and a sense of value and meaning in life. May they discover your love for them and your call to them to be weavers in the tapestry of your creation. I pray especially for…

I pray for the people I love, sharing with you my concerns about them and my hopes for them. I pray for…

I pray for peace in the parts of our world torn by war. I pray for the decision makers and the diplomats of the nations of the world, that they may resolve our conflicts without bloodshed, and for the military forces of our nations as they deter aggression. I pray for...

I pray...

Thanksgiving

O God, you have been gracious to me through all the years of my life. I thank you for your loving care, which has filled my days and brought me to this time and place. You have given me life and reason and set me in a world filled with your glory. You have comforted me with family and friends and ministered to me through the hands of my sisters and brothers. You have filled my heart with a hunger after you and have given me your peace. You have redeemed me and called me to a high calling in Christ Jesus. You have given me a place in the fellowship of your Spirit and the witness of your church. You have been my light in darkness and a rock of strength in adversity and temptation. You have been the very Spirit of joy in my joys and the all-sufficient reward in all my labors. You have remembered me when I forgot you. You followed me even when I tried to flee from you. You met me with forgiveness when I returned to you. For all your patience and overflowing grace, I praise your holy name, O God.[60]

Thank you for...

Dedication

God be in my head and in my understanding; God be in my eyes and in my looking. God be in my mouth and in my speaking; God be in my heart and in my thinking; God be at my end, and at my departing. [61]

Silence

Benediction

May the power and presence of Jesus Christ give you strength and wisdom as you go.

Scripture Passages for Meditative Reading or Group Study

Passages about listening prayer:
1 Samuel 3:1–18
Isaiah 6:1–8
Exodus 3:1–12
Genesis 6:1—8:22
Acts 9:1–18
Psalm 119:10–16
Jeremiah 33:1–3

CHAPTER 6

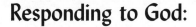

Responding to God:

For God alone my soul waits in silence.
Psalm 62:5

Great is the Lord, and greatly to be praised.
Psalm 48:1a

Here am I, the servant of the Lord; let it be
with me according to your word.
Luke 1:38

Bishop Lance Webb, in his book *The Art of Personal Prayer*, tells this story:

> The little son of a busy preacher pushed open the
> door of his dad's study, pulled a stool close to his
> father's feet and sat down with his round eyes fixed
> on his father's face. The father, who was behind in
> his sermon preparation, said rather impatiently,
> "Well, what is it? What do you want?" The big eyes
> grew wider in disappointment and the little boy
> said reproachfully, "I don't want anything. I'm just
> looking at you and loving you."[62]

Looking at and loving God is different from giving thanks to God. Your attention in thanksgiving prayer is on the gifts from God for which gratitude is due to God. The little boy in his father's study is not thinking about all of the provision his father makes for his life. His mind and heart are focused on who his father is and the love he feels for this man.

Three of the ways Christians pray involve looking at and loving God. One is silent, contemplative prayer. A second is praise that uses words and often music. A third is dedication, when we respond to God by giving back to God.

Contemplative Prayer

Weaving prayer into the tapestry of life is usually active. We ask, we confess, and we give thanks. We use words, thoughts, memory, imagination, reasoning, feelings, and will. Even listening prayer is active, involving us in "wanting to hear" and "paying attention." But prayer is not always doing. Sometimes it is just being.

The seventh day in the Genesis creation story portrays God as resting. After six days of doing, God spent a day just being. Contemplative prayer is a kind of resting while being alertly conscious of God's presence. It provides a unique dimension to the design of a life tapestry.

Contemplative prayer does not need words or even thoughts. It is silent prayer. You clear your mind and heart as much as possible and just open yourself to God. Psalm 46:10 can be structured as an invitation to this kind of quiet prayer:

> Be still and know that I am God
> Be still and know that I am
> Be still and know
> Be still
> Be

Bishop Desmond Tutu, in his book *God Has a Dream: A Vision of Hope for Our Time,* talks about the importance of stillness in his life. He says:

> Each one of us is meant to have that space inside where we can hear God's voice. God is available to all of us... We can hear God's voice most clearly when we are quiet, uncluttered, undistracted... I am deeply thankful for those moments in the early morning when I try to be quiet, to sit in the presence of the gentle and compassionate and unruffled One to try to share in or be given some of that divine serenity... People often ask about the source of my joy and I can honestly say that it comes from my spiritual life—specifically from these times of stillness. They are an indispensable part of my day.[63]

Contemplative prayer has a long history in Christian spirituality, going back to the desert fathers and mothers in the third century, to the mystics like St. John of the Cross, and to the practice of praying the Scriptures in the monasteries.

Centering Prayer

A small group of American monks in the twentieth century developed a contemporary version of contemplative prayer they named Centering Prayer. They were aware of the attraction of the meditation practices of the Eastern faiths and wanted Western Christians to know the presence of contemplative prayer in Christian history. Thomas Merton, Thomas Keating, and John Main recognized in their spiritual practice a treasure that could be shared.

Cynthia Bourgeault, who practices Centering Prayer and writes about it, describes her roots in the Quaker faith as her first introduction to contemplative prayer. She spent her first six school years in a

Quaker school where a "weekly silent meeting for worship was as invariable a part of the rhythm of life as schoolwork or recess."

> I can still remember trooping together, class by class, into the cavernous two-story meeting house and taking our places on the long, narrow benches once occupied by elders of yore. Occasionally, there would be a scriptural verse or thought offered, but for long stretches there was simply silence. And in that silence, as I gazed up at the sunlight sparkling through those high upper windows, or followed a secret tug drawing me into my own heart, I began to know a prayer much deeper than "talking to God." Somewhere in those depths of silence, I came upon my first experience of God as a loving presence that was always near, and prayer as a simple trust in that presence.[64]

She describes Centering Prayer as a simple method for reconnecting us with our natural aptitude for the inner life.

> What goes on in those silent depths during the time of Centering Prayer is no one's business, not even your own; it is between your innermost being and God; that place where, as St. Augustine once said, "God is closer to your soul than you are yourself."[65]

Centering Prayer is a possibility for everyone, but it is a discipline that takes time, nurture, and commitment.

A prayer by Juliana of Norwich, a fifteenth-century mystic in England, can serve as a call to contemplative prayer.

God, of your goodness, give me yourself; for you are sufficient for me. I cannot properly ask anything less, to be worthy of you. If I were to ask less, I should always be in want. In you alone do I have all.[66]

Praise

Philip Zaleski, author of *Prayer: a History*, describes how Centering Prayer has moved to a prayer of praise for him: "I have a sense of adoring this magnificent, inconceivable person who's given life to this whole world, and in that mixed rush of adoration and gratitude and thankfulness, I find the finest and best moments in my prayer."[67]

Praise is expressing your love for God. Praise celebrates who God is—God's glory, holiness, righteousness, justice, mercy, might, love, and creative power.

Praise can be very quiet, as in a moment of silent expression of awe and wonder at the miracle of the birth of a child. Praise can be very noisy, as in a large choir with orchestra singing Handel's "Hallelujah Chorus" with the full power of their musical resources. Praise can be expressed in ordinary language, as one expresses a compliment to an admired person. Praise is frequently set to music that can enhance the emotional power of praise. A popular hymn expresses praise as the singing of the soul.

> Then sings my soul, my Savior God to thee;
> How GREAT THOU ART! How GREAT THOU ART! [68]

Expressing our praise and love to God may be awkward at first. We may feel uncomfortable about praise, as if we are engaged in just "buttering up" God before getting to the petitions. We may find ourselves as a loss for words. What do you say? Another hymn expresses this sense of the inadequacy of ordinary words to express praise:

> God of the sparrow God of the whale
> God of the swirling stars
> How does the creature say Awe
> How does the creature say Praise[69]

For centuries, Christians have used the words "Alleluia" and "Hallelujah" from the Hebrew word for praise to transcend the limits of ordinary human language.

Frideric Handel has given the whole world a much-beloved expression of praise to God in his masterpiece *The Messiah* with his "Hallelujah Chorus." He combines specific descriptions (For the Lord God omnipotent reigneth) with ecstatic expressions of hallelujah.

Many hymn, anthems, and choruses in Christian worship express praise with these words. St. Francis of Assisi is credited with composing a hymn in 1225 that calls not only human beings but all creation to join in singing alleluia: "All creatures of our God and King, lift up your voice and with us sing Alleluia! Alleluia!" He then specifies parts of creation—the sun and moon, wind and clouds, morning and evening, flowing water and fire, and then, of course, people. All are invited to join him in alleluia.

Praise music is almost always joyful music. Praise and joy seem to belong together. St. Francis subtly shares an insight into the prayer of praise that is important for our spiritual journey. In his list of those he calls to sing alleluia, he mentions two categories of people: those who are tender hearted and forgiving, and people who bear pain and sorrow for a long time. It might strike the singer of this hymn as strange that St. Francis specifically calls on people who bear pain and sorrow for a long time to lift up their voices and sing, "Alleluia! Alleluia!" But praise is not just an expression of joy. It may also be a source of joy. The prayer of praise is not to be woven only into the bright and happy parts of the design of our life tapestry but in the dark, painful, and troubled parts as well. Joy can be a by-product of praise. Praise lifts one's attention from one's own situation to the wonder and beauty of God's presence and love. Looking at and loving God in a time of pain and sorrow can remind you that God is present with you, within you. You are not alone. The qualities and resources in the nature of God that call forth your responsive love are available to you in the worst of times. Remembering all of that as you sing alleluia can bring joy to your heart.

Prayer as praise plays a significant role in healthy spiritual growth and makes an important contribution to the tapestry of life.

Praise hymns and the Psalms are a wonderful source of meditation materials that tune the mind and heart to the joyous experience of praising God. We learn to express our love for God by hearing how others have done it. You can read some of these materials prayerfully and just add, "Me too."

Praise changes things. God can offer different possibilities where praise is expressed. Hope can appear on the scene. Sunshine can break through clouds. The tapestry of one's life can be brightened when praise is woven in. Your spirit may be better able to hear the ideal possibilities that are God's will for you when you respond to God with praise.

Dedication

The prayer of dedication says to God "My love for you is not just talk. I want to respond to you with commitment to live as you have created and are creating me to live. I want the tapestry of my life to reflect your will for me." The prayer of dedication says, "Let my life story be a subplot in the story you are telling." Using the image of weaving, the prayer of dedication says, "Let the tapestry of my life blend seamlessly into the broader tapestry of creation you are weaving." In a prayer of dedication, we give the gift of ourselves back to God.

Jesus began his model prayer for his disciples first with praise: "Hallowed by thy name". But immediately he expressed dedication: "Thy kingdom come, thy will be done." In other words, "My will is committed to your will. I want to be part of whatever you are doing."

Dedication is the ultimate response to God.

Listen to the words of some popular dedication prayers:

> Take my life, and let it be consecrated, Lord, to
> thee.
> Take my moments and my days; let them flow in
> ceaseless praise.
> Take my hands, and let them move at the impulse
> of thy love.
> Take my feet, and let them be swift and beautiful
> for thee.[70]

> Lord, I want to be a Christian in my heart,
> Lord, I want to be more loving in my heart,
> Lord, I want to be more holy in my heart,
> Lord, I want to be like Jesus in my heart[71]

Prayers of dedication do not have to be complicated or eloquent. Theologian John Powell has hung over his bathroom mirror a simple prayer that he uses daily: "Good morning, God. What do you have in mind for me today? I hope to be part of it."

There is an easy flow in the dimensions of prayer responding to God. Centering prayer leads to praise, which in turn calls forth dedication.

Mary's story in Luke's gospel illustrates the three dimensions of our human response to God. In Luke's report of the birth of Jesus, Mary got a request from God to become the mother of Jesus. She listened carefully. Her response was dedication and praise. Mary said yes and then said the beautiful words of praise known as the Magnificat (Luke 1:46–55).

Samuel Longfellow puts it all together in the first line of each stanza of his hymn "Holy Spirit, Truth Divine":

> Holy Spirit, (centering) Truth divine, (praise)
> dawn upon this soul of mine; (dedication)
>
> Holy Spirit, (centering) Love divine, (praise)
> glow within this heart of mine; (dedication)
>
> Holy Spirit, (centering) Power divine, (praise)
> fill and nerve this will of mine; (dedication)
>
> Holy Spirit, (centering) Right divine, (praise)
> King within my conscience reign. (dedication)
>
> He finishes with, "Be my Lord, and I shall be firmly bound, forever free."[72]

PRAYER PROMPTS 7
Responding to God

I come to prayer seeking to catch my breath
in the presence of your pure beauty.

Centering

For God alone my soul waits in silence.[73]

If you have been raised with Christ, seek the things that are above, where Christ is.[74]

Praise

Have you ever come on anything quite like this extravagant generosity of God, this deep, deep wisdom? It's way over our heads. We'll never figure it out.
Is there anyone around who can explain God?
Anyone smart enough to tell him what to do?
Anyone who has done him such a huge favor that God has to ask his advice?
Everything comes from him;
Everything happens through him;
Everything ends up in him.
Always glory! Always praise!
Yes. Yes. Yes.[75]

I praise you…

Confession

Most merciful God, I confess that I have sinned against you in thought, word, and deed, by what I have done, and by what I have left undone. I have not loved you with my whole heart; I have not loved my neighbors as myself. I am truly sorry and I humbly repent.[76]

Hear my confession…

If you confess your sins, God who is faithful and just will forgive you your sins and cleanse you from all unrighteousness.[77]

Meditative Reading of Scripture

Petition

Plant your word in my heart. Nourish it so that it may bear fruit in my life. Prune from me all that is not fruitful. I pray especially for…

Show me how I can use my wounds to make me a sensitive agent of your love for others who are wounded. I pray for…

I pray for guidance to see the way I should go in this perplexing circumstance…

I pray for…

Intercession

I pray for those whose needs are described in the news today...

I pray for those who are experiencing pain in relationships. Help them to find a way through hostility and bitterness and to break down the walls that divide and separate. I pray for...

I pray for those who have asked me to pray for them. I share with you their concerns and hopes as they have passed them on to me. I pray for...

I pray for...

Thanksgiving

O Supreme Lord of the Universe, you fill and sustain everything around us. With the touch of your hand, you turned chaos into order, darkness into light. Unknown energies you hid in the heart of matter. From you burst forth the splendor of the sun and the mild radiance of the moon. Stars and planets without number you set in ordered movement. You are the source of the fire's heat and the wind's might, of the water's coolness and the earth's stability. Deep and wonderful are the mysteries of your creation.[78]

I give thanks for the gift of life as part of your awesome creation...

Thank you for...

Dedication

Lord, I want to be a Christian in my heart. I want to be more loving and like Jesus in my heart.[79]

Silence

Benediction

Glory to God, whose power working in you can do more that you can ask or imagine.

Scripture Passages for Meditative Reading or Group Study

Passages about prayers of praise and dedication
    Matthew 14:22–23
    Matthew 6:1–6
    Psalm 96
    Psalm 19:7–10, 14
    Psalm 62:5–8
    Luke 1:26–55
    Romans 12:1–12

CHAPTER 7

Praying Together

For where two or three are gathered in my
name, I am there among them.
Matthew 18:20

In the early chapters of this book, I have described prayer as a solitary enterprise. One weaver uses one loom and creates one tapestry. One person praying has one life to weave into a life tapestry. But this is not the whole picture in Christian prayer. Christians pray with each other—always have, always will.

Each of us is responsible for weaving our own life tapestry. But as we weave, together we are also part of the larger tapestry of creation. This chapter looks at this larger picture of shared prayer and the role it can play in your weaving.

You may think of yourself sometimes as praying alone. But all Christian prayer is shared prayer. The threads of prayer that you weave into your tapestry now have come to you through generations of Christian people, some from the distant past and some from recent personal experience. You pray as part of that community, connected in the web of these shared threads even when you pray alone.

Jesus set the pattern. The first word of the Lord's Prayer—*our*—is plural. The model prayer he gave his disciples was plural from start to finish. Our father… give us… forgive us… deliver us. He expected his disciples to pray together.

The disciples learned this lesson well. Luke tells the story of the early days of the young Christian church in the New Testament book the Acts of the Apostles. Jesus was no longer physically with his disciples. They were leaderless and set adrift in an environment that was hostile to this new faith. In response to danger and threats from the Roman and Jewish authorities, they stayed together in an upstairs room "constantly devoting themselves to prayer" (Acts 1:14).

Christians claim as the birthday of the church an event that took place while the disciples were together. Luke tells the story of the day of Pentecost (Acts 2:1–42). The Holy Spirit descended on them like the rush of a violent wind with tongues of fire. They were all "filled with the Holy Spirit." A crowd gathered, Peter preached, and before the day was over, about three thousand people were baptized. The Christian church was launched in a small community that "constantly devoted themselves to prayer." On another occasion the disciples were praying, and "when they had prayed, the place in which they were gathered together was shaken; and they were all filled with the Holy Spirit and spoke the word of God with boldness" (Acts 4:31). This was not a one-time event. Praying together was a regular part of their lives.

Before long, the disciple Peter was put in prison for teaching the faith. Luke reports that the people of the church "were praying earnestly to God" for him when the doors of the prison were opened and he was set free. He left the jail and went to a place where "many had gathered and were praying" (Acts 12:1–12).

With the prayers of the people and the work of the Holy Spirit, the brand-new Christian church was off and running. More than two thousand years later, we are still at it.

Why Do We Pray Together?

Why did Jesus tell us to pray together? Why is it not enough to communicate with God quietly and privately? Why does the church continue to provide opportunities for us to pray with each other?

1. For starters, being a Christian is not an individual matter. One is baptized not into a solitary religious experience, but into a faith community—the church. Praying together the prayers of the church connects us with each other, our heritage, and the universal church. Praying together the prayers that have been shaped and tested over time in Christian worship helps individual Christians to grow into the faith of the church. These prayers become part of who we are at the deepest levels of our being.

2. Christians also pray together because we believe there is power in shared prayer. God does not listen more carefully to the prayers of a great congregation in a huge cathedral than to the prayer of a patient in pain in a hospital bed. But our prayers give God an opening to work in us God's will. When more than one of us prays for the same thing, God has more to work with in answering the prayer. One has to wonder how the birthday of the church at Pentecost might have happened if Jesus' disciples had not been in one room praying together.

3. Praying together performs an educational function in the Christian community. We can learn to pray and expand our ideas about prayer by being around other people who are praying. Children, young people, new Christians, all of us, grow in the practice of prayer by hearing the words, observing the body language, and feeling the spirit of someone else's prayer. We can enrich our private prayer by what we learn in shared prayer.

4. Praying with others is a practical way to express caring and compassion and a way to "bear each other's burdens." Praying for yourself and others by yourself is important. But having someone else praying with you or for you, especially if you can hear the prayer, can be a source of great encouragement, strength, and hope. As a pastor, I learned how valuable it is simply to listen to someone's concerns and then to express his or her wants and needs and hopes to God in prayer. I have had my own tears turned to a smile when someone has done that for me.

5. Praying when we are together is also important to our life as Christians because it sends a message. Sharing prayer with others is a witness to the value we give to prayer. When we begin and/or close a meeting with prayer, invite people to meet together for prayer, or schedule family prayer time, we make a statement that prayer is important.

   My niece, Margaret Rowlett, who is a Quaker and who serves on a national committee for that community, recently shared an experience. Her committee met on a conference call of members around the nation. Their meetings always begin with a time of silence for centering and direction. The quiet time together was essential, so committee members silently held their phones for this prayer time. Her story was a witness to me to the value they experience in silent prayer.

6. A pattern of praying with others encourages us to pray. The habit of regular church attendance on Sundays guarantees that you will pray at least once a week. A prayer group or family prayer time calls you from other activities on a schedule.

7. Since most of us don't sing alone, praying with others provides a unique opportunity to sing our prayers. The combination of words and music in hymns, responses, anthems, and choruses moves prayers to deep places in our souls. I have led worship services in care facilities with people suffering from dementia. They may not recognize family members or even be able to carry on a conversation, but when a pianist begins to play one of the old hymns of the church, some of them can sing many of the words with warmth and fervor and shining faces. When I express my amazement to the staff, they smile and nod. Those sung prayers are woven into the tapestry of their lives in a part of their brains not damaged by their diseases and seem to continue to nurture their spirits. Who knows how important those resources of prayers set to music and tucked into that broader range of brain cells can be for the rest of us?

How Do We Pray Together?

The Upper Room, a United Methodist publisher of spirituality resources, once made a survey of about four thousand churches. They asked how people prayed together in their congregations and invited them to share stories about their experience. Respondents described twenty-two different settings in their replies, and shared enthusiastic stories about how important these experiences of praying with other Christians are for the people involved.

Weekly congregational worship services were the most frequently mentioned time and place for praying together. Here kindred spirits can connect with each other to share in a wide variety of dimensions of prayer. The order of service for Christian worship gives structure for a meaningful flow—centering, praising, confessing, giving thanks, asking, listening, and dedication.

Every week millions of Christians gather in congregations all over the world:

- to sing prayers of praise and thanksgiving with harmonized voices;
- to encourage and strengthen each other in intercession for the needs of the world;
- to confess not only individual sins but social sins in which we are all involved;
- to receive the bread and wine of communion with the community of faith;
- to dedicate financial offerings in a shared plate placed on the altar;
- and to hear other voices praying the Lord's Prayer as an experience of our oneness in Christ.

With the radio, television, Internet and mobile media, it is easy to pray with a congregation without being physically present. But adding your voice to the singing, sharing the physical touch of the handshake of welcome, hearing the word of peace personally spoken, and receiving the consecrated elements of bread and wine require you to be there. Your physical presence in the congregation also enhances the community and encourages and supports other people. We pray with others not only for what we receive but for what we give.

Prayer groups were reported in the Upper Room survey as the second most popular way people pray together in contemporary churches.

Intercessory prayer groups are everywhere, and they come in a wide variety of sizes and formats, with local adaptations. The focus is on asking prayers, but many include personal sharing, praying the Scriptures, prayer songs, and silence. Marjorie Suchocki describes the powerlessness an individual may feel in the face of the problems of the world:

> After all, how can I, an individual living in a suburb,
> have any effect upon the rising homicide rate in

the city? How can I, a mere individual, affect the issues that place nations in warring postures? What can I do about the pervasive "isms" in our society that single out some for ill-treatment? And how on earth can I address some issues of organized crime, or economic structures that ensure poverty and homelessness for so many? Whatever the issue may be that drains well-being from society, the only clarity about it is that it is too big for me, and I have neither the power- nor the will - to address it. Powerlessness becomes apathy.[80]

Individuals may feel overwhelmed by just the needs of members of one congregation. But if a group shares the assignment of intercession, God receives from the prayers of several open hearts resources for responding with possibilities for a new future.

The kind of intercessory prayer group most frequently reported in the survey invites prayer requests from the congregation and meets weekly to pray together about the concerns raised. There is strength in numbers and in the encouragement of company.

Covenant prayer groups commit to pray for each other. In my minister's group mentioned in chapter 3, we had commitments to each other that defined the group. We met monthly for one and a half hours. Everything said was confidential. Each person answered the question, "How goes it with your soul?" Everyone prayed for everyone else. Part of the covenant was that we did not give advice or express personal opinions. We simply supported each other in prayer. Some covenant groups commit to practicing certain spiritual disciplines and report to each meeting to hold each other accountable.

Centering Prayer groups were reported by several churches. A block of silent time (usually twenty minutes) was combined with study and discussion on Christian spirituality using books and other resources. One person was responsible for watching the time and ringing a chime or bell to end the silence. Centering Prayer groups meeting regularly helped members sustain the practice.

Family prayers seem to be surviving the hectic schedules of busy twenty-first-century families. The survey did not report the patterns used but simply noted that this is happening. Historically this has been a central occasion for nurturing children in Christian faith and practice. A childhood memory for me is the reading the Upper Room devotional booklet every day as the family gathered around the table for a meal.

Prayer retreats continue to be a popular setting for praying together. A retreat is usually an extended time, an overnight or a weekend, at a quiet place where you can focus attention on your spiritual journey. Individuals can go on a prayer retreat, but group retreats offer a chance to talk with other people about faith and to share prayer in a relaxed and unpressured environment. The retreat schedule may include study, small group discussion, individual prayer time, group worship, relaxation, and recreation. Participants usually go home inspired, refreshed, and renewed.

Healing services are a regular part of the ministry of some churches. The New Testament letter of James instructs the members of the early church: "Are any among you sick? They should call for the elders of the church and have them pray over them, anointing them with oil in the name of the Lord... so that you may be healed" (James 5:14, 16). Christians are still following this direction.

The public image of faith healing has suffered from the publicity given to charlatan faith healers. *The United Methodist Book of Worship* speaks to the resulting climate of distrust:

> A Service of Healing is not necessarily a service of curing, but it provides an atmosphere in which healing can happen. The greatest healing of all is the reunion or reconciliation of a human being with God. When this happens, physical healing sometimes occurs, mental and emotional balance

is often restored, spiritual health is enhanced and
relationships are healed. [81]

Praying for healing can take place anytime and anywhere
Christians pray with one another.

I once belonged to a prayer group that decided to end one of our
meetings with a visit to the home of our pastor, who often met with
us. He was confined to bed after back surgery. He was a very active,
energetic person, and this restricted routine was difficult for him.
We stood around his bed and listened to his story of struggle with
the pain and physical limits. Then each of us laid a hand on him and
individually prayed for healing in his body, mind, and spirit. Our
prayers were heartfelt and sincere. A few weeks later, my eyes filled
with quick tears when I saw him bound up the steps at the church
with a broad smile on his face.

The healing ministry of Jesus that is carried on by the Christian
church includes concern for spiritual, mental, and emotional health
as well as physical health. We don't stop praying for or with someone
when they receive a terminal diagnosis. In the face of death, spiritual
life can rise to new levels of health and wholeness. Reginald Mallett,
in a sermon at Lake Junaluska, North Carolina, pointed out that God
continues to offer ideal possibilities for each day's weaving of our life
tapestry even when we confront death. He said:

> Sometimes the human body does not respond to
> any kind of therapy. However, when the container
> in which we live is hopelessly flawed, the contents
> can be wonderfully whole.[82]

We can pray together for this healing.

The Internet opens the possibility of praying with millions of
other people. One website, www.sacredspace.ie, provides guides
for daily prayer based on a different passage of Scripture for each
day, with on-screen guidance. Their format of prayer prompts is

designed for a ten-minute prayer time, but the time is flexible. You can move from section to section in the prayer when you are ready with a simple mouse click. The creators of the website, Irish Jesuits in Dublin, provide translations into eighteen languages. You can pray with a global community.

The Upper Room offers an online daily prayer guide with a Scripture passage, a meditation, and a prayer. Many other prayer resources are available on the web.

Prayers at the beginning and/or end of *committee meetings, board meetings, and conferences* bring the thread of prayer into the weaving Christians are doing together. These prayers are openness both *to* God and *with* God—acknowledging God's presence, inviting God's guidance and direction for the task at hand, and committing to God's will the progress made.

Prayer in solitude provides the opportunity for interacting with God about the unique tapestry you are weaving. But private prayer needs the balance, guidance, and inspiration of community prayer. Praying alone and with others provides wholeness in the experience of Christian prayer.

PRAYER PROMPT 8
Praying Together

I come to prayer to join my human love
in a chorus of wonder and praise.

Centering

For where two or three are gathered in my name, I am there among them.[83]

Like the sun that is far away and yet close at hand to warm me, so God's Spirit is ever present and around me. Come Creator, into my life. I live and move and have my very being in you. Open now the window of my soul. [84]

Praise

Come! Come! Everybody worship with a prayer or song of praise!
Come! Come! Everybody worship! Worship God always!
Worship and remember the Lord's unending care,
reaching out to love and help people everywhere.
Worship and remember that God is like a light,
showing you the way to go; ever burning bright![85]

I praise you for…

Confession

Eternal and gracious God, I have wandered away from your presence like a lost sheep. I have been absorbed in my own agenda and doing my own thing. I have done things that are contrary to your will. I have left undone things that I ought to have done, and I have done things that I ought not to have done.[86] Hear my confession…

Forgive me and direct my feet back to the path to which you are calling me.

If you confess your sins, God, who is faithful and just, will forgive you your sins and cleanse you from all unrighteousness.[87]

Meditative Reading of Scripture

Petition

God, grant me the serenity to accept the things I cannot change, the courage to change the things I can, and the wisdom to know the difference.[88]

Help me to hear in your Word a word for our time. Show me how the ancient, eternal truth still has power to transform life now…

I pray for protection from all that might hurt or destroy me…

I pray for…

Intercession

I pray for those who live with fear because of violence in their communities or in their homes. Help them to find paths to safety and peace. May they know relief, justice, and healing. I pray for…

I pray for the poor, the hungry, and the homeless. May they be remembered and their needs met out of your bounty as we serve as stewards of your gifts. May human compassion improve their condition and community action remove the causes of their suffering. I pray for...

I pray for the leaders of the nations of the world, that they may live with integrity, choose what serves the common good, seek peace, and protect the earth's resources. I pray for...

I pray for...

Thanksgiving

God of love, I thank you for the multitude of gifts with which you have blessed me. I am grateful for your presence both in the days of health and strength and in the times of grief and pain. I thank you for the community of your Church, and for welcoming me there in my baptism as your beloved child. I thank you for providing everything I need to live the life to which you have called me.

Thank you for...

Dedication

Spirit of the living God, fall afresh on me.
Melt me, mold me, fill me, use me.
Spirit of the living God, fall afresh on me.[89]

Silence

Benediction

The grace of the Lord Jesus Christ be with your spirit. [90]

Scripture Passages for Meditative Reading or Group Study

Passages about praying together:
> Matthew 18:20
> Acts 1:12–14
> Acts 2:1–42
> Acts 12:1–12
> James 5:14–16
> Luke 5:17–26
> Luke 7:1–10

CHAPTER 8

The Difference Prayer Makes

Do not worry about anything, but in everything
by prayer and supplication with thanksgiving let
your requests be made known to God.
Philippians 4:6

The television camera focused on Mother Teresa of Calcutta. She was seated in a private jet writing a letter. The narrator described how she handled the business of her worldwide religious order of one hundred thousand members with handwritten correspondence delivered by regular mail. She was hitching a ride to look at some of her work in another Indian city. A bemused male voice from another part of the plane asked, "Where do you get all of your energy, Mother?"

She lifted her head. Her tranquil face was framed by her blue and white habit. "That's why we go to the Mass," she said. "We start the day with Him and we end the day with Him." Members of her order work with the lepers, the indigent dying, the orphans, the poor of India. Those who live in the mother house in Calcutta are expected to be back from their day's work in time to be present at the evening worship. "We are not social workers, you know," she explained.

In her tapestry of life, the thread of prayer was woven into the design of every day. Her life opened the way for God to make a powerful difference in the world. Her prayers affected for good not only the people on the streets in Calcutta, but the nation of India, the worldwide Christian church—the whole world.

You also create an opening for God's will to be done when you pray. You move beyond simple self-centered considerations. Personal needs and desires may be the original reason you pray, but when you put your concerns out in prayer, you involve God. The prayer may be changed, you may be changed, and the world may be different—all because you prayed. You begin with your personal welfare and find yourself caught up in God's will for the good of the whole creation.

Prayer Makes a Difference to the One Who Prays

What does this difference look like? Paul, in the first New Testament letter to the Corinthians, talks about three qualities of the Christian life that can serve as a summary of God's will for us: faith, hope, and love. When you pray, you open the way for God's spirit to nurture in you these three qualities so they become an integral part of the tapestry of your life.

Faith

If a human friendship is to survive and grow, communication and interaction are necessary. I need to know you to trust you. The only way we can get acquainted is by trusting each other enough to reveal ourselves. A little trust makes the first steps of friendship possible. This initial acquaintance can open the way for more trust, which can lead to deeper friendship. So it is with prayer and faith. Faith expressed in a simple prayer opens the way for the Spirit to nurture in you growing faith. As your trust in God deepens, your experience of prayer can expand.

Karen Armstrong points out that we don't wait for faith before we pray. We start out with praying, and faith can grow:

> To expect to have faith before embarking on
> the disciplines of the spiritual life is like putting
> the cart before the horse... Faith is the fruit of
> spirituality.... Prayer is not born of belief and
> intellectual conviction: it is a practice that creates
> faith.[91]

Thomas Merton pointed to this interdependence between prayer and faith in remarks to a group of monks at a California monastery. Michael Terry, a member of that group, reported that Merton advised:

> Start where you are and deepen what you already
> have and you realize that you are already there.
> Everything has already been given to us in Christ.
> The trouble is that we don't know what we have.
> All we need is to experience what we already
> possess. The problem is that we don't slow down
> and take time to know it.

I have kept a prayer journal over the years, often writing out my prayers. When I go back to pray these prayers again, I am frequently amazed at what has happened in the interim. Many prayers no longer fit. Some have been answered, often in ways that had not occurred to me when I was praying but that were much better solutions than I could have imagined. Some prayers embarrass me. In response to God's call in my life, I have grown beyond what now seem to be petty, self-centered, and immature requests. When I observe the change, my faith in God expands and deepens, enabling new dimensions of prayer.

If I had not prayed in the first place, my faith would have stayed mainly in my head. Faith might have been an intellectually defensible creed or a tradition I chose to accept rather than being personal experience.

Prayer is an expression of faith that can open your life to growing faith. The weaving of one thread of prayer into your tapestry may lead to the weaving of many threads of prayer that will transform the design from what it would have been without prayer/faith.

Hope

The Spirit also has an opportunity to nurture hope in your weaving when you pray.

Henry Nelson Wieman in his book *The Wrestle of Religion with Truth* describes a streetcar that operated in Los Angeles in the early part of the twentieth century. At one point along its route it climbed a hill. He reports:

> The hill is so steep that the car cannot use an overhead trolley. It is lifted by a steel cable which runs endlessly beneath the car and between the rails. But the car does not move until it is connected with the cable in the proper manner. The car stands still until its passengers are in. Then a clamping mechanism closes down upon the cable and the car is lifted to the top of the hill.

Worship, he says, is the way we clamp down on the cable. When you pray, you discover that you are not alone. You are in God, and God is in you. You do not have to climb your hills in your own strength alone. You can tap into God's resources for your life. The resources of prayer are a source of hope.[92]

The apostle Paul describes this hope as "the peace of God which surpasses all understanding." He writes to the Philippians:

Do not worry about anything, but in everything by prayer and supplication with thanksgiving let your requests be made known to God. And the peace of God, which surpasses all understanding, will guard your hearts and your minds in Christ Jesus. (Philippians 4:6–7)

In his sermon at Pentecost, Peter quoted his ancestor King David, referring to the hope given by awareness of God's presence. Eugene Peterson expresses with enthusiasm Peter's sense of hope in his paraphrase *The Message: The Bible in Contemporary Language.*

> I saw God before me all the time.
>> Nothing can shake me; he's right by my side.
>> I'm glad from the inside out, ecstatic;
>> I've pitched my tent in the land of hope.
>> You've got my feet on the life path,
>> with your face shining sun joy all around.
>> (Acts 2:25–26, 28)

A person who weaves a tapestry of life hopefully is more likely to be open to the new possibilities offered by God than is a person who is burdened with discouragement, locked in the grip of fear or guilt, or inhibited by doubts. Communion with the "almighty to create, almighty to renew" is a channel for the sustenance of hope, a source of strength and energy, a medium through which the Spirit can prepare you to receive possibilities you might not otherwise perceive.

In prayer, we can discover that we have more than the resources with which our past has equipped us for facing the hills we have to climb.

Love

When you pray, you give the Holy Spirit a chance to nurture love in you. God's will is that all of us grow in three kinds of love: 1) a healthy kind of self-esteem or respect and appreciation for the unique persons we have been created to be; 2) a corresponding esteem for our human brothers and sisters combined with a willingness to care for them; and 3) a deepening love for and commitment to God. In prayer, God calls you to all three kinds of love.

Love for Yourself

Church members occasionally object to the inclusion of a prayer of confession in the order of worship for the congregation. "It makes people feel bad," they say. "Confessing our offenses and our negligence stirs up guilty feelings and contributes to low self-esteem. People come to church to feel better, not to feel worse."

Christian confession, however, is a means of grace. When you confess who you are to the One who already knows you and loves you as you really are, you have a chance at self-esteem grounded in personal integrity. God's acceptance and forgiveness do not say that everything you have done and left undone is all right. They say you can pick up from here and move on. Freed from the burden of guilt, you can live with your real, sinful self. You can accept yourself because God accepts you. You can value yourself. If God prizes you, how can you not do the same?

Prayers of confession open the way for God's forgiveness to do its cleansing work in your life and set you on a path to healthy self-love.

Love for Others

Prayers of intercession can grow your love for others. When you pray for other people, you join your spirit with God's good will for them. You may have all sorts of feelings about the others for whom you pray. Being candid about that is a good place to start the prayer. But if you are genuinely open *to* God as well as *with* God, you will be exposed to God's unconditional love and eternal good will for this person. God's spirit will call you to share God's perspective and genuine long-term good will as well.

When you pray for another person, your prayer may be

answered with a fresh insight about what you can do to contribute to that person's well-being. As you act on that insight, expressing your love, your love for that person can grow.

Jesus taught his disciples to pray for their enemies. He understood that this would give the Holy Spirit a chance to show them ways to deal constructively with the conflict or enmity. Acting on such insights opens the way for improved relationship and moves us in the direction of love.

At the least, the prayers of intercession stretch us beyond self-centeredness and widen the horizon of our concern. As we open ourselves to God's love for other people, some of God's compassion can be contagious. Mother Teresa, for example, said that she saw Christ dying in the gutters of Calcutta. When we give God a chance, we may find ourselves sent out as agents of divine love.

Love for God

You give the Holy Spirit an opportunity to increase in you love for God when you pray. You open yourself to more profound comprehension of who God is when you take time for praise. An expanded and clarified vision of God has enhanced power to evoke devotion.

Expressing gratitude can lead to increased love for God. You intensify your awareness of what God does when you celebrate God's grace and God's gifts to you by saying, "Thank you."

Love for God will blossom when you experience God's responsive love in answer to your prayers for yourself and others. Change can come to the quality of your life when you dedicate yourself and what you have to God's service. This difference can warm your heart and nurture your love for God.

Just taking time to be consciously aware of God's loving presence can lead you to obedience to the great commandment: "You shall love the Lord your God with all your heart and with all your soul and with all your mind" (Matthew 22:37).

God's ideal possibilities for our lives find an opening through which they can enter the life weaving process when we pray.

Prayer Makes a Difference to the World

Weaving prayer into the tapestry of your life makes a positive difference to the world around you. Everything you do is significant because it changes the way the world is in the moment when you act. That change may be for good or for ill. The world is blessed by the presence of more faith and hope and love as your life is moved toward these qualities when you pray. These changes in you make a difference to the way the world is.

Beyond that, your prayers make a difference in what God can do in the world. What God can offer you changes when you pray. For example, God can offer you new possibilities when you leave behind a crippling burden of guilt. New life opens before you. Your vision of possibilities for yourself, others, and the world can be transformed when you listen for God's word to you. People who listen for what God believes the world can be are more likely to be engaged in serving God's purposes than those who don't see beyond their own self-interest. God can guide you into improved relationships when you pray for your enemies. God can nurture gratitude and hope in you when you give thanks.

A person growing in faith and hope and love gives God resources that God did not have for serving God's good will in the world. Your openness to God creates a channel through which God can work God's loving will in the world.

Mother Teresa's sisters were not social workers, she said. Social workers may be making the world a better place every day, but her sisters saw their service as a channel for God's love. They knew they needed to be in that conscious relationship with God that we call prayer every day. They were receiving gifts of grace from God as they prayed. They were giving themselves back to

God to be used in response to these gifts of grace. Their prayers had given God a resource God otherwise would not have had.

Most questions about prayer that I hear have to do with those times when all you can do about something is to pray. Is there any point in praying when you can't see anything you can do or that God can do through you? Does your prayer make a difference when the situation is too big or too far away for you as one person to be involved? Should we just "stick to our knitting" and pray for things for ourselves and others close to us?

Jesus began the model prayer with the big view, His opening petition is for the whole earth. "May your kingdom come, your will be done on earth as it is in heaven." He prayed for everybody and everything. Jesus must think that this is valuable. This is his prayer guide for all disciples. We can take him at his word and do as he did.

All of creation is connected in God. God is a part of all creation. We meet each other in God. Our prayers for others and for the world make a difference in the interconnectedness of all reality.

How God answers prayer is beyond our thoughts, and God's ways are not our ways. But we can trust that our prayers give God more to work with in influencing the world for good. An unending parade of witnesses to the power of prayer moves across the centuries of recorded history.

The larger tapestry of all creation is changed as we weave prayer for each other and our world into our individual life tapestries.

Prayer Makes a Difference to God

Our prayers give God resources for doing God's work in our world. Our prayers open our life tapestries to the gifts God would give us, and our life tapestries make a difference to God.

Some people are so bold as to suggest that God is enriched by our sharing in prayer and that as we express praise and thanksgiving and share ourselves in confession, petition, intercession, and dedication, as we rest in God's presence in contemplation, we even contribute to God's pleasure! Is there any wonder Christians have understood prayer to be a part of God's will for our lives?

PRAYER PROMPTS 9
The Difference Prayer Makes

I come to prayer to gather anything
that is true and holy within me.

Centering

Do not worry about anything, but in everything, by prayer and supplication, with thanksgiving let your requests be made known to God.[93]

I gratefully receive the gift of prayer and the grace it brings into the depth of my being.

Praise

God of all peoples, you are the true light illumining everyone. You show me the way, the truth, and the life. You love me even when I am disobedient. You sustain me with your Holy Spirit. I rejoice in your presence with me.[94]

I praise you for...

Confession

Heavenly parent, who by your love has made me, and through your love has kept me, and in your love would make me perfect, I humbly confess that I have not loved you with all my heart and soul and mind and strength, and that I have not loved others as Christ has loved me. Your life is within my soul, but my selfishness has hindered you. Hear my confession...

Forgive what I have been; help me to amend what I am; and in your Spirit direct what I shall be; that you may come to the full glory of your creation in me and in all people, through Jesus Christ our Lord.[95]

Meditative Reading of Scripture

Petition

Nurture in me your gifts of faith and hope and love so I may be filled to overflowing and pass these gifts to others...

I trust that you have given me all I need to live the life you are calling me to live. Help me to discover these gifts and to use them to your glory...

Teach me to pray, Lord. I want to know the riches of your gift of love in the relationship of prayer. Guide me as I reach out in trust to listen and to speak to you, to wonder at the miracle of prayer, and to warm my spirit in the glow of your presence...

I pray for...

Intercession

I pray for my family. May our common life be marked by mutual honor, respect, and forgiveness. Touch our painful memories with your grace, and teach us patience in bearing with each other. I pray for...

I pray for those who are dealing with the crises of this day. May they find wisdom and courage and strength adequate for meeting their challenges. May they serve the common good and move the world in the direction in which you are calling us. I pray for...

I pray for the church. May all who have been baptized into its fellowship be filled with your spirit and faithful in love and good works. I pray for...

I pray for...

Thanksgiving

Now thank we all our God with hearts and hands and voices, who wondrous things has done, in whom this world rejoices; who from our mothers' arms has blessed us on our way, with countless gifts of love, and still is ours today.[96]

I give thanks for...

Dedication

Holy Spirit, Truth divine, dawn upon this soul of mine;
Word of God and inward light, wake my spirit, clear my sight.
Holy Spirit, Love divine, glow within this heart of mine;
Holy Spirit, Power divine, fill and nerve this will of mine;
Holy Spirit, Right divine, King within my conscience reign;
be my Lord, and I shall be firmly bound, forever free.[97]

Silence

Benediction

The peace of God, which surpasses all understanding, will guard your hearts and minds in Christ Jesus.[98]

Scripture Passages for Meditative Reading or for Group Study:

Philippians 4:6
Isaiah 55:6–12
Matthew 22:37–40
Acts 2:25–28
1 John 4:7–21
John 15:9–12
1 Corinthians 13:1–13

Endnotes

1. Adapted from worship resources by Bruce Prewer, with permission.
2. Martin Luther. *The Table Talk* (London: Bell, 1978), 155.
3. Psalm 42:1.
4. From an African American spiritual.
5. Adapted from the hymn "Joyful, Joyful, We Adore Thee" by Henry Van Dyke (1907).
6. Based on "Morning Prayer II" from *The Book of Common Prayer,* 101.
7. From an African American spiritual.
8. Jean-Pierre De Caussade. *Abandonment to the Divine Providence,* 36.
9. Alfred North Whitehead. *Process and Reality,* 346.
10. Revelation 21:5.
11. Selected lines from Psalm 8 from Eugene Peterson, *The Message: The Bible in Contemporary Language,* 918.
12. Adapted from "A Service of Word and Table I" in *The United Methodist Hymnal,* 6.
13. Adapted from "Prayers of Confession, Assurance and Pardon" in *The United Methodist Hymnal,* 891.
14. John Oatman Jr., 1897.
15. Adapted from Lesser Doxology, third and fourth centuries.
16. Mother Teresa in Gattuso. *Talking to God,* 28.
17. Friedrich Heiler. *Prayer,* 363.

18. Desmond Tutu in Abernethy and Bole, *The Life of Meaning*, 133.
19. Title of hymn by Walter Chalmers Smith (1867). *The United Methodist Hymnal*, 103.
20. De Caussaud, *Ibid.*
21. Thomas Kelly. *Testament of Devotion*, 29.
22. Used with permission.
23. Desmond Tutu in Bob Abernethy and William Bole. *The Life of Meaning*, 133.
24. John Cobb and David Griffin. *Process Theology: An Introductory Exposition*, 41.
25. From worship resources by Bruce Prewer.
26. John B. Cobb, Jr., in a message to friends August 22, 2008.
27. Psalm 46:10.
28. From an African American spiritual.
29. Adapted from *The United Methodist Book of Worship*, 462.
30. Adapted from 1 John 1:8–9.
31. Adapted from I John 1:9 in Peterson, *The Message*.
32. Based on a prayer attributed to Richard of Chichester (1293).
33. Traditional South African prayer.
34. Jane E. Vennard. *Intercessory Prayer*, 47.
35. Hunter, *Preventive Prayer and Meditation*.
36. Quoted from sermon by Rob Blackburn at Central United Methodist Church in Asheville, North Carolina. Used with permission.
37. Luke 11:9.
38. Isaiah 40:31.
39. Selected lines from the hymn "I Sing the Almighty Power of God" by Isaac Watts (1715).
40. Adapted from *The Book of Worship for Church and Home*.
41. Adapted from *The Book of Common Prayer of the Church of England (1922)* as quoted in *The United Methodist Book of Worship*, 467.

42. Selected lines from the hymn "For the Fruits of This Creation" by Fred Pratt Green.

43. Selected lines from Dag Hammerskjold. *Markings*, 100.

44. Based on Ephesians 3:20.

45. Psalm 106:1.

46. Adapted from Psalm 43:3.

47. Based on themes from Psalm 103:1–14.

48. Adapted from "Contemporary Prayers for Public Worship" by Caryl Micklem (1967) as quoted in *The United Methodist Book of Worship*, 480.

49. Based on prayer from *The Book of Common Order, Scotland* (1940):*25*, quoted in *The United Methodist Book of Worship*, 553.

50. Adapted from *The Kingdom, the Power and the Glory (1933)* as used in "For the Mind of Christ" in *The United Methodist Book of Worship*, 514.

51. Philippians 4:23

52. Rick Warren sermon at Saddleback Church in Lake Forest California, "Can You Hear Me Now?" Sermon 3 in a series on "How to Receive an Idea from God" March 20–21, 2004.

53. *Ibid.*

54. Dietrich Bonhoeffer. *Life Together*, 94.

55. Reuben Job. *Journey Toward Solitude and Community, Participant's Workbook*, 45.

56. John 4:24, author's paraphrase.

57. 1 Samuel 3:9.

58. Acts 2:25–26, 28.

59. Adapted from *Gates of Prayer: The New Union Prayer Book (1975)* as used in *The United Methodist Book of Worship* (Jewish Prayer for Forgiveness, U.S.A., 20th century), 478.

60. Adapted from the "Covenant Renewal Service" in *The United Methodist Book of Worship*, 290.

61. Sarum Primer, medieval prayer.

62. Adapted from Lance Webb. *The Art of Personal Prayer*, 10–11.

63. Desmond Tutu, "Stillness," from *God Has a Vision of Hope for Our Time* by Desmond Tutu and Douglas Adams as quoted in Gattuso, *Talking to God: Portrait of a World at Prayer*, 129.

64. Cynthia Bourgeault. *Centering Prayer and Inner Awakening*, 4.

65. *Ibid.*, 6.

66. "The Sufficiency of God" by Juliana of Norwich, England, fifteenth century. *The United Methodist Hymnal*, 495.

67. Philip Zaleski, "The World's Prayers," in Bob Abernethy and William Bole, *The Life of Meaning*, 121.

68. Selected lines from the hymn "How Great Thou Art" by Stuart Hine.

69. Selected lines from the hymn "God of the Sparrow, God of the Whale" by Jaroslav J. Vaida.

70. Selected lines from the hymn "Take My Life and Let It Be" by Frances Havergal.

71. African American spiritual.

72. Selected lines from the hymn "Holy Spirit, Truth Divine" by Samuel Longfellow (1864).

73. Psalm 62:1.

74. Colossians 3:1..

75. Romans 11:33–35 from *The Message: The Bible in Contemporary Language* by Eugene Peterson.

76. Adapted from "Prayers of Confession, Assurance, and Pardon" in *The United Methodist Hymnal*, 890.

77. 1 John 1:9.

78. Attributed to "New Orders of the Mass in India" as quoted in *The United Methodist Book of Worship, 556.*

79. From an African American spiritual.

80. Marjorie Hewitt Suchocki. *In God's Presence,* 80.

81. "Healing Services and Prayer" in *The United Methodist Book of Worship,* 613–14.

82. Reginald Mallett, from a sermon preached at Lake Junaluska, North Carolina, July 27, 1988. Quoted in James K. Wagner, *An Adventure in Healing and Wholeness,* 57.

83. Matthew 18:20.

84. Adapted from 1987 United Methodist Clergywomen's Consultation Resource Book, 61. Quoted in *The United Methodist Book of Worship*, 473.

85. Selected lines from "Come, Come, Everybody Worship" by Natalie Sleeth in *The United Methodist Book of Worship*, 199.

86. Based on *The United Methodist Hymnal*, 891.

87. Adapted from 1 John 1:9.

88. The Serenity Prayer, attributed to Reinhold Niebuhr.

89. Hymn "Spirit of the Living God" by Daniel Iverson (1926).

90. Philippians 4:23.

91. Karen Armstrong, "Creating Faith," in John Gattuso, *Talking to God: Portrait of a World at Prayer*, 25.

92. Henry Nelson Weiman. *Wrestle of Religion with Truth*, 70-71.

93. Philippians 4:6.

94. Adapted from *The United Methodist Book of Worship*, 118.

95. Adapted from "Prayers of Confession, Assurance and Pardon" *The United Methodist Hymnal*, 892.

96. Selected lines from the hymn "Now Thank We All Our God" by Martin Rinkhart.

97. From the hymn "Holy Spirit, Truth Divine" by Samuel Longfellow (1864).

98. Philippians 4:7.

Bibliography

Abernethy, Bob, and William Bole. *The Life of Meaning.* New York: Seven Stories Press, 2007.

Bonhoeffer, Dietrich. *Life Together.* New York: HarperCollins Publishers, 1954.

Bourgeault, Carolyn. *Centering Prayer and Inner Awakening.* Lantham, MD: Cowley Publications, 2004.

Cobb, John B., Jr., and David Ray Griffin. *Process Theology: An Introductory Exposition.* Philadelphia: Westminster Press, 1976.

De Caussade, Jean-Pierre. *Abandonment to the Divine Providence.* Garden City: Doubleday, 1975.

Gates of Prayer: The New Union Prayer Book.1975. Central Conference of American Rabbis and Union of Liberal and Progressive Synagogues. New York: CCAR,192 Lexington Avenue, 10016.

Gattuso, John, editor. *Talking to God: Portrait of a World at Prayer.* Milford, NJ: Stone Creek Publications, 2006.

Hammarskjold, Dag. *Markings.* (Trans.by Lief Sjoberg and W.H. Auden). New York: Alfred A. Knopf, Inc., 1964.

Heiler, Friedrich. *A Study in the History and Psychology of Prayer*. Tr and ed by Samuel McComb. London: Oxford University Press, 1932.

Hunter, Allan. *Preventive Prayer and Meditation*. Ashland, OH: Disciplined Order of Christ, n.d.

Job, Reuben. *A Journey toward Community and Solitude: Participant's Workbook*. Nashville, TN: Abingdon Press, 1982.

Keating, Thomas. *Intimacy with God: An Introduction to Centering Prayer*. New York: The Crossroad Publishing Company, 1994.

Kelly, Thomas. *Testament of Devotion*. New York: Harper & Brothers, 1941.

Magee, John. *Reality and Prayer*. New York: Harper & Row, Publishers, 1957.

Micklem, Caryl. *Contemporary Prayers for Public Worship*. London, England: SCM Press, 1968,

Prewer, Bruce. www.bruceprewer.com. Sunbury, Australia.

Suchocki, Marjorie. *In God's Presence*. St. Louis, MO: Chalice Press, 1996.

The Book of Common Prayer. New York: The Church Hymnal Corporation, 1986.

The Book of Common Order, Scotland. Oxford, England: Oxford University Press, 1940.

The Book of Worship for Church and Home. Nashville, TN: The Board of Publication of the Methodist Church, Inc., 1965.

The United Methodist Book of Worship. Nashville, TN: The United Methodist Publishing House, 1992.

The United Methodist Hymnal. Nashville, TN: The United Methodist Publishing House, 1989.

Vennard, Jane E. *Intercessory Prayer: Praying for Friends and Enemies.* Minneapolis, MN: Augsburg, 1995.

Wagner, James K. *An Adventure in Healing and Wholeness.* Nashville, TN: Upper Room Books, 1993.

Warren, Rick. Sermon series at the Saddleback Church, in Lake Forest, CA, on *How to Receive an Idea from God.* Sermon 3, "Can You Hear Me Now?" March 20–21, 2004.

Webb, Lance. *The Art of Personal Prayer.* Nashville, TN: The Upper Room, 1977.

Weiman, Henry Nelson. *The Wrestle of Religion with Truth.* New York: The Macmillan Co, 1927.

Whitehead, Alfred North. *Process and Reality.* New York: Free Press, 1978.